D0324355

MARK RUTLAND

Word of Life Series

RESURRECTION

receiving and
releasing God's
greatest miracle

CREATION HOUSE
A STRANG COMPANY

RESURRECTION by Mark Rutland
Published by Creation House
A Strang Company
600 Rinehart Road
Lake Mary, Florida 32746
www.creationhouse.com

Unless otherwise noted, all Scripture quotations are from the King James Version of the Bible.

Cover design by Rachel Campbell

Library of Congress Control Card Number:
2005936907
International Standard Book Number: 1-59185-951-4

First Edition

05 06 07 08 09 — 987654321
Printed in the United States of America

ACKNOWLEDGMENTS

I AM PERSUADED that not even the best among us dare to pray for their just desserts. Shakespeare asked, "If we got what we deserve, who should 'scape whipping?" Certainly not I. I do not want what I deserve. I want grace.

The irritatingly convenient forgetfulness of the arrogant suffers them to believe they can do all without help and deserve all without gratitude. I loathe the thought that ingratitude might hide among the vast catalog of my other sins.

What great grace God showed me in my wife, Alison. She is not the woman I deserved. Early on, I dated the woman I deserve, and I shudder to contemplate my fate if I had gotten her. In my Alison, God's grace me-ward is marvelous indeed. Now I must ask myself, "What is Alison's sin that God gave me to her, that I might have her. I got grace; she got me. That hardly seems fair."

This book, as indeed all my books should be, is dedicated to Alison. It is in her life, more than in anyone else's, that I have seen the reality of our resurrected Lord. We are raised with Him to newness of life, and that "newness" in her life has been a blessing to mine.

At a practical level, I admit, without reluctance, that one of the points in this book came to me through her. It was Alison who made precious, in a teaching, Jesus' question, "What things?" I hope she is happy with how I have treated that thought in *Resurrection*.

My gratitude also goes to my son, Travis, who envisioned the Five Smooth Stones series and who has been its major motivator. Dr. Gordon Miller, as always, has been a faithful and diligent line editor and Karen Maldonado, the typist. To them and to all who directly or indirectly contributed to this project—thank you.

CONTENTS

Preface . . . . *vii*

Part 1: On the Resurrection of Christ

1 The Body of Death 1

2 Theologians, So Called 10

3 What Things? 22

4 First Fruits 32

5 Why Not Judas? 45

6 The Culture of Death 58

Part 2: On Raising the Dead

7 Life and Death in the Land
of Spamalot 74

8 Life or Law 88

9 Cemetery Maintenance 96

10 The Dead in Christ 106

PREFACE

I N *FORREST Gump*, the intellectually impaired hero walks with his beloved Jenny to see the house she lived in throughout her sexually abused childhood. At the very sight of the dilapidated, abandoned shack, she begins to throw stones at the windows until she collapses in sobs.

Forrest poignantly and pitiably observes, "I suppose sometimes there just aren't enough rocks."

In the face of the monstrous Goliath looming before him, young David put five rocks, in his shepherd's wallet. They were the proper ammunition, carefully selected for shape and weight, to arm his sling for battle. With the first one, the giant fell at his feet, and the other four were never used.

Much has been made of those smooth stones. Why five, for instance? Some have suggested they were for Goliath's brothers. Perhaps. It seems more likely to me, however, that the extras were the prudence of an experienced sharpshooter who knew that even the best marksman occasionally misses. Some would make that a lack of faith, but even if David doubted his aim, he hardly doubted God.

The point is that all of us occasionally need more than one rock. This book is the final "stone" of the five I offer in this series. May this one, and the other four, be a blessed addition to your personal armory.

Satan's strategies are many, but the weapons of our warfare are sufficient. I pray that when you face a Goliath of satanic empowerment that your first stone topples him like a domino. If not, choose another stone, and another, and keep firing until he drops.

I have made a sentence, not the only one possible, of the five smooth stones in this series. Put this sentence and the stones in your bag and fire at will. Satan would have you believe that your past is your future, that you cannot change or win or overcome. Five smooth stones in the sling of a warrior are the answer to that lie.

Nevertheless, may your *Dream* of *Holiness* come true in the *Power* of the *Resurrection*.

PART 1

ON THE RESURRECTION
OF CHRIST

CHAPTER 1

THE BODY OF DEATH

GRIEVING WOMEN, for women are always the ones to care for the dead, prepare a body for the tomb. They wash it, and as they do, they weep. Theirs are tears of both sorrow and horror. Their friend, a young man, *and* the husband of none of them, is dead, and they are grieving. Also, they weep in horror at the sight of Him. He is mangled, the massacred handiwork of experts. Their tears are also the tears of the truly horrified, of the grief-stricken who have seen the nightmare of human sadism for themselves. So they weep as they wash the body of their friend and wrap it in clean linen.

It is nearly sundown, and their law says that the body must be laid to rest before sundown on the very day it dies. The women will return, they say to each other. After the Sabbath they will unwrap the body, anoint it with embalming oils, and rewrap it in linen. There is no time now. The sun is sinking quickly, and the law must be obeyed.

RESURRECTION

Their friend is dead, horrifically dead. They do not understand why He had to die, especially in such unspeakable agony. They do not know what will become of them. Where will they go now? Home? Can they even go back to such an ordinary existence? They do not know the answer to any of these things.

All they know is that their friend is dead. His body, washed and wrapped for entombment, will soon begin the process of decomposition to which all bodies eventually fall prey. That is the one thing they know. His story will end as His body decays. Death claimed their friend, and no one, not even He, has an answer to its finality. His spirit gone, His body will go as well; it will just take longer to leave.

*　　*　　*

Decomposition is an ugly process. Odious in the extreme, nauseatingly, stupefyingly odious, it assaults our senses as well as our emotions. Tidy phrases such as "ashes to ashes and dust to dust" are mere euphemisms for that final degradation of the human body, the return to the soil from which it came. Flesh, having given up the ghost, does not give up its form easily. Bodies yield slowly to the dirt. The killing fields of history have taught us one thing; the stench of dead bodies is an incredible odor, impossible to hide.

Having slain and hidden Polonius, Hamlet tells King Claudius, "You shall nose him as you go up the stairs…"

All that follows death is so repugnant, so horrifying, that it makes the mind and soul shrink from considering it. Still, bodies cannot be left strewn about. No one wants to deal with death, but death not dealt with causes more death. After natural disasters, such as the 2004 tsunami in Asia, the risk of disease dictates mass response to mass death.

The journey of the redeemed soul is serene and leads to heaven. The bodies of even the saintliest among us face a very different passage; from life, through death, and on to decay. The destination of the spirit is heaven. The end of the body is earth.

The ancient Egyptians perfected the embalmer's art to fend off, not death, but decay, yet their tombs have yielded plenty of proof that their mummified dead, even their royalty, were not spared. Wisps of hair and cloth, thousands of years old, cling to bodies remarkably "preserved," but they are preserved as what raisins are to grapes, wrinkled leather pouches emptied of life.

Every culture deals with its human remains in its own way. The Comanche on the North American plains put dead bodies on wooden platforms open to the elements and carrion birds. In India, cremation is the more common method. At funerals in the United States, well-paid professionals encase embalmed, made-up corpses first in expensive coffins, and then into steel crypts. Whether by fire or by decay, whether slow or fast, the end result is the same: ashes to ashes, dust to dust.

*   *   *

The end of Shabath dawned brilliantly, a beautiful spring morning with a refreshing coolness in the air. The radiant sky above the Jordan blazed orange, promising fevered heat by noon day. The city began to stir; its voice muffled, still sleepy, rose in muted tones to start the week. Cook fires began to send their plumes aloft, straight up in the windless air for what seemed like miles.

It was the perfect morning. It would have been, anyway, had he not been blind to it all. Sludge, thick and black, oozed down the inner walls of his mind in gruesome contrast to the morning. Guilt-ridden, his tortured mind played and replayed the ugly scenes of the last few days. Nothing would stop the pictures and silence the voices, certainly not this pristine dawn or the wild, sweet melody of the morning birds.

"Peter." John's voice had a soothing quality. It always did. But nothing could soothe Peter now. Nothing. "Peter, the women are here with ... well, you better listen to what they have to say."

"John, I can't ... I ... look at me. You take care of it. I'm finished. I should've ... maybe Judas was right."

John's eyes brimmed with compassion. He loved this big man, and to see him so utterly shattered grieved him. "Peter, don't say that. Don't ever say it. Come on. Come with me and hear the women out. You need to hear this. Come on. They're inside, and you have to hear them out."

Peter allowed the smaller man to guide him back inside. "Is it more bad news, John? I don't think I can bear anymore."

"Bad news?" John had the strangest look in his eyes. "I'm not sure, Peter. Maybe, maybe not. They've already been out to the Master's tomb."

Peter stopped in his tracks. "What's wrong?"

"I don't know. I'm not sure. Here they are now. Hear them out; then you tell me."

The women rushed toward Peter, their faces flushed with excitement. Peter moaned softly. Women confused him. He hardly understood his own wife, and this Magdalene was beyond him. Hysterical women. He would hear them out, but he was already certain it could not be good news. The Master was dead, slaughtered actually. What good news could there be? After death, especially that kind of death, there is no good news.

In the distance, inspired by the golden dawn, a rooster crowed, and Peter shivered. That sound, that horrible sound. Whatever the women had seen at the tomb or thought they had seen, it could never wipe that sound from his mind.

*   *   *

It is impossible for us to grasp the pain and despair of Christ's disciples in the hours following the passion. Peter had denied the Messiah, Judas committed suicide, and the others scattered in loneliness and disillusionment. They had hoped this was He for whom Israel waited. They had almost convinced themselves of it.

Then in one long, terrible night and the torturous day that followed, He in whom they had believed *and* all their hopes of glory were gone, crucified, dead, and buried.

It is clear that none of them, not even the closest of His followers, had any real expectation of a physical resurrection. If they had, they would not have been so surprised when it happened. Surprised? Flabbergasted is more like it. Indeed, the stupendous unlikelihood of a resurrection made it difficult for them to believe and even clouded their vision in the face of reality. On multiple occasions people with whom Jesus had enjoyed an intimate relationship for several years were unable to recognize Him.

A case could be made that the resurrected Christ looked different from the Jesus of Nazareth with whom they had lived and traveled. Perhaps, but once they *recognized* Him, once their eyes were opened, not one person commented that He looked different. The postresurrection Jesus did not glow in the dark or sprout wings. In fact, what confused the disciples was not that the resurrection changed Jesus' appearance, but that it did not. One does not expect, cannot even contemplate, the prospect that a dead man would meet with them, explain scripture to them, and even break bread with them. The naturalness of the resurrection was what temporarily blinded them to Him.

Certainly, Jesus had more than hinted at His resurrection. "Destroy this temple, and in three days I will raise it up" (John 2:19). In this statement, as in many of His others, however, there was an apparent double meaning that left both His critics and His followers confused. It was only after the resurrection that His disciples understood with certainty which temple would be "raised."

> Then said the Jews, Forty and six years was this temple in building, and wilt thou rear it up in three days? But he spake of the temple of his body. When, therefore, he was risen from the dead, his disciples remembered that he had said this unto them; and they believed the scripture, and the word which Jesus had said.
>
> —JOHN 2:20–22

The resurrection of Jesus' body is critical to the Christian faith. Indeed, without it there is

nothing to have faith in. For that reason, the resurrection of Jesus has been assailed by forces on
every side of His followers from the very morning it happened. The guards posted to watch the
tomb of Jesus were put there because of resurrection talk among His followers and others. Had
He said He would rise again? The Romans and
the Sanhedrin were not sure what He had said,
but they could be sure He would not rise. The
order was given to seal the tomb and set guards.
Thus began the coordinated attack of religion
and politics on the greatest truth in the universe.

CHAPTER 2

THEOLOGIANS, SO CALLED

D ID JESUS mean it literally? Perhaps He referred only to the great resurrection, in which, by the way, the Pharisees fully believed. Regardless, the religious leaders could take no chances on His followers stealing the dead body and faking a resurrection. Guards were posted and the tomb was sealed (Matthew 27:62–66). Both proved useless.

Those same guards were bribed (with "large money," Matthew says) to perjure themselves by claiming that just such a conspiracy had indeed happened, that the dead body had been stolen by zealots and a fraud was about to be perpetrated (Matthew 28:11–15).

Liberal theologians have relentlessly continued the attack for two thousand years. Some have claimed that the resurrection was not physical but communal. In other words, they would have us believe that Jesus' followers wanted so badly for Him to be alive that in the space between them they just made it so. These "theologians," so called, claim that Jesus' resurrection was not bodily but cultural and emotional, a shared hope so desperately held among them that it became "real" in their hearts, but not in His body. *In 1967, one writer, Hugh Schonfield, even went so far as to endorse the testimony of the bribed guards in a book called The Passover Plot.* According to Schonfield, the vinegar-soaked sponge lifted to Jesus on the cross was actually filled with a drug powerful enough to simulate death. He further claimed that Joseph of Arimathea rescued Jesus before He died, later resuscitating Him for "postresurrection" appearances.

Why all the desperate effort to discredit the bodily resurrection of Jesus? Because His resurrection is all our hope, the ground of all true faith in Christ. He died and rose again. He did not nearly die, He did not rise from the dead merely in the minds of His followers or in the hearts and affections of His friends. His resurrection was not an idea or a wish. It is a fact. His scars still visible, He rose physically.

The grave could not hold Him. Death had been done to death, and that is the hope of our faith. In his first letter to the church at Corinth, Paul labeled the resurrection as the gospel in which we stand and by which we also are saved.

> Christ died for our sins...and...was buried, and that he rose again on the third day according to the scriptures.
> —1 CORINTHIANS 15:3–4

Paul goes on to frame the importance of the resurrection in no uncertain terms.

> Now if Christ be preached that he rose from the dead, how say some among you that there is no resurrection of the dead? But if there be no resurrection of the dead, then is Christ not risen: And if Christ be not risen, then is our preaching vain, and your faith is also vain. Yea, and we are found false witnesses of God; because we have testified of God that he raised up Christ: whom he raised not up, if so be that the dead rise not. For if the dead rise not, then is not Christ raised: And if Christ be not raised, your faith is vain; ye are yet in your sins. Then they also who are fallen asleep in Christ are perished. If in this life only we have hope in Christ, we are of all men most miserable.
> —1 CORINTHIANS 15:12–19

The scriptures to which Paul refers are the Old Testament, of course, which certainly tied resurrection to the Messiah. Later in that same chapter of 1 Corinthians, Paul even references both the Feast of First Fruits and Genesis.

> But now is Christ risen from the dead, and become the firstfruits of them that slept. For since by man came death, by man came also the resurrection of the dead. For as in Adam all die, even so in Christ shall all be made alive. But every man in his own order: Christ the firstfruits; afterward they that are Christ's at his coming.
> —1 CORINTHIANS 15:20–23

Testified to by many eyewitnesses, the resurrection of Christ was not some addendum to the story added by medieval monks five hundred years later. The resurrection was written of in all the Gospels in substantial, complementary detail.

Furthermore, the fierce opposition from both religious and political leadership lends weight to the veracity of the resurrection. If Jesus' resurrection was but a fraud put forward by blue-collar conspirators from Galilee, it is doubtful that such substantial bribes would have been paid after high-level negotiations were carried out between the high priest and the governor himself. Such powerful forces of darkness are not marshaled to oppose bizarre myths unlikely to outlive the perpetrators themselves. Indeed, modern books claiming that the resurrection was a hoax perpetrated by the misguided or the power hungry are part of the satanic effort to hide hell's greatest defeat behind a cloud of accusation. It will not work. Pilate could not seal the tomb. The soldiers could not guard it. The Sanhedrin could not pay enough bribes to stop the news of Jesus' resurrection from spreading. And faithless unbelievers cannot write enough evil books to put Him back in the tomb.

The greatest of all the doctrines of Christianity quickly became its sweetest greeting and response. Shared among believers, sometimes whispered to each other in settings that could have meant death, the encoded words spoke of a hope, a shared eternity that neither Rome nor religious opposition could destroy.

Christ is risen.

He is risen indeed.

*   *   *

Peter gawked at her, a volatile mixture of emotions surging through him. Hope, an almost ferocious hope like nothing he had ever before experienced, welled up within him. Guilt, fear, and even some inexplicable anger churned together in his soul until he was unsure whether to be furious with the woman or delighted, whether to embrace her or slap her.

"What do you mean empty?"

"Empty, Peter. What do you think I mean? Empty."

"His body was gone?"

"Yes, I'm trying to tell you. Gone."

"Where, Mary?"

"What's the matter with you? I don't know. We went early to anoint the body. The stone was rolled back, so I went in."

"All the way in?"

"All the way in."

"And?"

"And nothing. Empty. They have taken the Master's body. Why, Peter, why would they do that? Wasn't killing Him enough? Why torture us by hiding His body?"

Peter and John exchanged glances; then,

without a word, he turned and ran. As always the slimmer, smaller John outran the big man. Peter had not won a footrace since boyhood.

John arrived at the tomb first but stood outside peeking in like a timid child at the rabbi's study door. Never wanting for boldness, Peter, winded and gasping for breath, plunged through the opening into the large tomb's weeping chamber. There ahead of him and to the left was the carved stone ledge where the corpse had been laid in its linen shroud. The winding cloth was there, neatly folded, but the body of their friend was missing.

"He is not here," Peter whispered.

"No."

Peter turned back to John, his eyes full of questions. "What does it mean?"

"I don't know, Peter. At least I'm not sure yet."

"Sure of what?"

"I'm sure of nothing, Peter. Except one thing. He is not here. That is all we know for now. Where He is, I do not know. But He is not here."

*   *   *

Who can share another's grief? We may sit with a friend at the funeral home or embrace weeping parents who have just lost a child, but we

16

cannot truly share their grief. We cannot because it is theirs alone. The stupidest thing we can say to the grieving is, "I understand." To be with the bereaved, to listen, to sympathize and comfort is the best we can do. What we cannot do is lift grief from their shoulders and place it on our own.

The weight of grief can be staggering. It's an unbearable burden that can drag entire lives and families into a lightless pit of loneliness and pain. Suffering from grief, folks may act irrationally, saying and doing things that are contrary to their character. Grieving mothers, having lost a child, may lash out at their living children, wounding them deeply or even driving them away and giving death a double victory.

Adding guilt to grief can create a cocktail of emotional destruction. One woman told me that the last words she ever spoke to her little boy as he left with his father were a promise to spank him when he got home. When father and son were killed in a car crash only moments later, those words haunted her for decades. She did not cause the crash, and the child does not remember the words in heaven. The burden is hers, not his, and she is still struggling to bear it.

Another woman, in an argument with her

father, told him to drop dead. He did. At her feet. Years of counseling and mountains of medication have hardly dulled her pain.

What if, for the sake of fear, the fundamental human instinct for self-preservation or for, say, money, one were to betray a friend, even cause his death? That is a nightmare for the soul, a wrenching dream of horror from which many might never awaken. Some in such darkness might "take arms…and end it," as Hamlet said. Others, waiting, hoping against all hope, might somehow find the strength not to end the pain but to endure it. They peer at the eastern horizon, not so much believing as longing to believe that the sun also rises.

*   *   *

She tarried by the tomb without any apparent reason to do so. The men, not believing her, had come to see for themselves and, having seen, had left. She was no longer the pulse-pounding beauty she had been in her teens. A carefully cultivated aura of sensuality had surrounded her then, the very fragrance of sexuality and the brazen promise of sex. That was gone, thank God, banished by the One she now mourned. In its place was a calm, mature grace. She was not a beautiful woman, but a handsome one with intelligent eyes and even features. Taller than most Jewish women, she intimidated many men. She was used to it, to being rebuffed, spoken to harshly, even ignored by men struggling to deal with her attractiveness, charm, and intelligence.

Only Jesus seemed to relate to her without that between them. He had talked to her without an edge in His voice, had never looked at her with lust or looked away in embarrassment, but had listened attentively and answered without condescension. She let her head covering slip to her shoulders, and the morning sun dallied among the silken highlights of her hair. She brushed away her tears and fought back anger. He would not have wanted the anger. She knew that. But this, this disgusting theft, was the last straw. She, a woman without influence or power, had been forced to watch as the only pure man she had ever known was tortured and killed. She had also watched as men, men who belittled her for being the woman she was, refused to be the men they were supposed to be. Judas, whom she had never trusted, had sold Jesus out. His suicide gave her no grief at all. Peter, whom she had never liked, was wallowing in guilt. Usually decisive, even bold, he was staggering, and she could see it. Even John, brilliant, contemplative John, seemed unable to find any meaning in all this nightmare. He did not rebuff her questions. He simply did not respond.

Now this, this unspeakable abomination had been the final indignity. Having plucked Jesus from her life, slaughtering Him like a sheep, why had they stolen His body? Could they not even allow Him to be properly buried? Her life had been filled with men, and this merely confirmed what she had always known. They were weak at best and monstrous at worst.

At a noise behind her, not exactly a noise, but a movement, actually, she spun on her heel. Fully expecting to find soldiers, her heart racing, she saw instead a single man. Without a uniform, in the clothes of a common working man, He was most likely the gardener. Indeed, who else would be here in this garden so early? Seeing no malice in His eyes, she was emboldened to demand answers, but she forced herself to ask humbly, hoping to keep any feminine hysteria or strident anger from her voice.

"Please, sir, what have you done with Him?

Just tell me where His body is. Do they still fear Him? Can I not even anoint Him for burial? Please, I beg of you."

With a single word, her own name, the man in the garden turned her world upside down. At that word, that simple name so softly spoken, her eyes were opened, her entire being, in fact, opened as never before to an incredible flow of light and joy.

"Mary." Just that. Her name on His lips, and the darkness fled before the brilliance of His gaze.

How could she have been so blind? How could she not have recognized Him? It was Jesus. The same eyes. The same face and beard and hair and voice. The same, yet different. He was alive. Standing right in front of her, as alive as He had ever been, perhaps He looked no different at all. She lunged toward Him. Nothing in the world mattered, nothing in all of history, hers or the world's…nothing mattered in the least but Him.

"No, Mary. Touch me not. Not yet. I have not yet been to the Father. Go, tell Peter and the others to meet Me in Galilee. Go now. Let Me do what must be done. Then I will embrace you all."

CHAPTER 3

WHAT THINGS?

THE MOST important word Jesus ever spoke to Mary was her name. It is so for all of us. The Lord of life, risen from the dead, with cosmic duties still to perform, met her and called her by name. That was all the healing from grief she would ever need. Relationship was restored by the resurrection. Jesus' conquest of the grave was personal to her. The sinful world was thus redeemed. The law was satisfied, the grave was conquered, and death was defeated. But in that moment, there in the early morning, in the garden of a rich man, the resurrection was about none of those things...not as far as Mary was concerned. He was alive to *her*. He was with her, comforting her, calling her by name.

When in our darkest hours, when in grief or pain or loss, His resurrection becomes real, it will be real because it becomes personal. Jesus did not rise from the dead just for humanity at large. He rose for you, *to* you. Staggering under some crushing weight, reeling from a body blow that has left you struggling to breathe, listen for your name upon His lips. Let the great doctrine of the resurrection, which is a glorious biblical truth, become experience, personal and redemptive.

The resurrection happened. That is a fact. Yet historical fact must somehow translate into personal comfort. When you fully embrace the reality that the resurrected Christ is alive *to* you and *for* you uniquely, that He knows your name and your pain and meets you in the lonely garden of your grief, His resurrection begins its healing work in you.

"Mary." Just that. All Jesus said was her name, and the woman of Magdala was healed, her gloom dispelled. He was not just raised *from* the dead. He was raised *to* her. He was still her friend, still knew her name, and even on the way to His mission in the Temple of the Eternal Presence, He paused to speak to her.

Many years ago when I was a young pastor, an elderly woman in my church lost her husband of more than fifty years. His death left her not only grief-stricken but also fearful. Now alone on their remote farm, every *wind-blown* branch scraping across her window at night struck terror in her heart. Her children begged her to sell the old

23

home place and move in with them. Indeed, she expressed to me that she was tempted in some ways to do so. Fear, especially at night, tortured her. She had never spent the night alone in her entire life. Not once. Moving from her father's farm to her husband's, she had lived in the shelter of their protection. Now alone, elderly and vulnerable, fears racked her. We prayed about it often, but she found little comfort.

One Sunday morning she arrived at church absolutely radiant. The night before, a fearsome thunderstorm had knocked out power to much of the area, including her farm. Having wept herself to sleep, she awakened with a terrible start, sensing that she was not alone in the room. The storm had passed and a full moon illumined her upstairs bedroom. She reported to me that Jesus was seated in her husband's favorite rocker, rocking slowly and smiling at her.

Stunned and not knowing what to say, she blurted out, "My husband is dead, and I am so afraid."

She told me that He spoke to her in a warm tone that comforted her deeply. "I know, Ethel. He is with me, and I am with you. Go back to sleep. I am here."

Her eyes shining with delight, she reported that she had instantly fallen back to sleep. She said it was the first deep and satisfying night's sleep she had experienced since her husband's death and that she had awakened, not just refreshed, but filled with peace and happiness.

"What do you think, Pastor? Was it a dream, or was it real?"

I stammered for an answer, but before I could come up with anything, she laughed and answered herself.

"What conceivable difference could it make? Whether it was a dream or in the flesh makes no difference. He is alive. He will sit by my bed every night and watch over me. I will never be afraid, ever again."

The resurrection was no longer doctrine to her. Theology can be cold comfort. It is His presence in the garden, His voice speaking our name that vanquishes fear and exiles gloom from our lives. I am always amazed at those who are wiling to dismiss such moments in the lives of others as fantasy or even fabrication. If Jesus is risen, and He is, why should He not be risen indeed to a frightened widow?

One of my professors in seminary, on more

than one occasion, ranted in bitter sarcasm about a certain hymn that he despised, could hardly even bear to hear sung. He denounced it as mere sentimentalism. To this day I remember one particularly harsh accusation he leveled at the old hymn.

"It is maudlin," he claimed. "It badly personalizes the resurrected Christ in a way that even sounds possessive. This pathetic song takes the resurrection and turns it into a personal, even romantic, experience."

I should hope so. His point was that the truth of the resurrection is *true* whether I "feel" it or not. Yes, of course, but "feeling" His presence cannot be wrong. My professor was the one that was wrong. The old song is a good one when sung in quiet joy and with a calm, well-comforted faith by those whom He has touched and called by name.

> I come to the garden alone,
> While the dew is still on the roses;
> And the voice I hear, falling on my ear,
> The Son of God discloses.
> And He walks with me, and He talks
>   with me,
> And He tells me I am his own,

And the joy we share, as we tarry there,
None other has ever known.
—"IN THE GARDEN"
BY CHARLES AUSTIN MILES,
PUBLIC DOMAIN

In an attempt to keep believers from being
bounced around by emotion, theologians tend
to overcorrect. Resurrection faith is not mere
emotion, but neither is it meant to be emotion-
less theology gutted of joy and stripped of all
delight. The cold, perfect marble of well-carved
doctrine is of small comfort. Mary needed, not
wanted, but needed Jesus to be there, to meet her
and call her name. The dawn reunion of Mary
Magdalene and her beloved Master has great
importance to the theology of the church.

But what about Mary? Was there no importance to her? Mary Magdalene's was not just a
nice story. She was a person. It was to the person Mary, to the hurting, confused, grieving
woman that she was, that Jesus appeared and
spoke. In that moment she was not thinking
about theology or how this would be a great
addition to the New Testament. He was alive,
and He was alive to her.

RESURRECTION

*   *   *

As they walked, their corporate confusion followed them like a cloud. Inside that cold fog of unknowing they found no hopeful insights and shared no wisdom. They simply trudged on toward Emmaus asking each other the same questions and expecting no answers. What lay behind them in Jerusalem made no sense. The hopeful, exciting, miraculous bubble in which they had lived for the last three years had burst with tragic consequence, and their grief was gradually giving way to a numb search for meaning.

Their friend was dead. In just these few days, they were already coming to grips with the brutal fact. It was the unreasonableness of it all that engulfed them now. Past denial, even beyond anger, they waded on toward Emmaus through a thickening slough of *whys*. They did not want Caesar dead or Pilate crucified. They did not ache for revenge. They longed for answers.

Eyes on the roadway, they saw that with each step puffs of dust arose to cloak their sandaled feet. Muffled by confusion they heard each other's voices as from a distant room, muted, disembodied mutterings that hung suspended in the muddy air. No one noticed when the stranger fell in with them, or at least, no one cared enough to pay Him any mind until He insinuated Himself into their grieving incomprehension of the nightmare they had witnessed.

"What are you talking about?"

"Are you the only one in Jerusalem, in all of Israel, who hasn't heard about the terrible things that just happened in Jerusalem?"

"What things?" the stranger asked, and somehow the question, something about the way he listened, burst the dam, and out poured their pain-drenched *story* of their friend, of how He died in agony, and of their own deep confusion. They spoke of hopes cruelly dashed. Their pain poured out of them, and as they talked, they, not the one crucified, became the story. They talked not so much about the passion of their Master as about the confusion that gripped their own souls.

After a long while, the stranger began to talk, and His grasp of the Scriptures was remarkable. This stranger, so obviously a working man like themselves, explained the Scriptures like no rabbi they had ever heard. But before He talked, He listened and waited, hearing them, looking from face to face as they told Him the terrible story.

RESURRECTION

His explanations were medicine, yet at the beginning, it was not His answers but His listening that began to heal their wounded, tortured souls. He listened, not interrupting them, not arguing or dismissing their pain. His open ears, His sensitive, listening ears and tender eyes so filled with compassion, comforted them as they loosed the torrent of their words. Answers came, beautiful, clear, and full of hope, answers they needed. They soaked them up, drank them in like men dying of thirst. But before He explained anything He listened. They could not get enough of what He had to say, but only after He heard all that they had to say.

*   *   *

The resurrected Christ comes not just to teach but to listen. The most poignant and powerful question asked on the road to Emmaus was not theirs, but His. "What things?" What things, indeed. He listened while they told Him His own story from their limited and pain-filled perspective. They told Him of His own arrest, torture, and death, until gradually the point of the story shifted from Him to them.

He could have rebuked them. He might well

have said, "Look, I understand 'these things.'" Instead, He asked, and then waited as they went through it all from His arrest to their confusion. "What things?" He asked.

In the resurrection of Christ we have a blessed confidence that the One who knows every detail of our story better than we listens better than anyone. It is the resurrection that gives us hope of being heard in heaven. Raised from the dead, Christ walks the Emmaus road not just to explain what we cannot *understand*, but to hear our every wounded word without rebuke.

CHAPTER 4

FIRST FRUITS

A N UNCONSCIOUS child was rescued from the bottom of a swimming pool. Her terrified parents and concerned onlookers watched in agony as a lifeguard expertly gave her mouth-to-mouth. When water gurgled up and, coughing and sucking in breath, the girl sat up and opened her eyes, the crowd cheered and her parents wept with joy.

She was *resuscitated*. Where there was no breath, breath came again. One might say she was more dead than alive. Unable to breathe, her little lungs flooding with water, she would have been dead soon enough. But she was not dead.

A friend of mine bought a dilapidated house that I thought beyond hope. Unwilling to discourage him, I said nothing, but I was certain it was a bad investment. The pathetic old shack was better suited for the wrecking ball as far as I could see. My friend was undeterred. One year later an absolutely gorgeous home stood in its place, which, by the way, he sold for nearly three times his total investment. I, of course, claimed that I had been confident from the beginning that the project would succeed. That is *renovation*.

In the state where I live, a church experienced such a sudden surge of power that it virtually became a new church. Almost overnight, a local congregation was transformed into a ministry center to which people trekked from all over the world. Now, that congregation is slowly morphing yet again into whatever a church must become in the wake of such a blaze of glory. That transition will be interesting to watch, but in all three stages it was a church, not a corpse.

A dead body, a corpse, is a spiritless shell, the quickly decaying remains of a life. It is not in a state of suspended animation or of impending death. A renovation will not help, and resuscitation is too little, too late. Even revival is too effete a word. A Broadway play, ignored and unperformed for years, may experience a "revival." Some form of architecture long out of favor may find a "revival" of sorts, and some slumbering church lacking power and liveliness may burst into a raging conflagration. Those are *revivals*.

A revival is not a resurrection. Fresh life, new life, perhaps better or more life comes in a revival, but that cannot be construed as a resurrection. Resurrections reverse total death, not spiritual decline, or plateaued growth. Death and decay will not be renovated, resuscitated, or revived. Resurrection is to renovation as childbirth is to a trip to the beauty shop.

The resuscitation of a near-drowned child is doubted by none and applauded by all. A renovated house delights the neighborhood, enhances property values, and challenges the faith of no one. Even church revivals, for all their controversy and chaos, are recognized as what they are—temporary moves of God stirring the dormant to new life.

Only a resurrection, the resurrection of Christ, could outrage doubters, scandalize intellectuals, and launch a faith in eternal life sufficient to change the world and the sinful hearts of men.

*   *   *

"Now watch," her father told her. "Here comes the priest. I love this part."

She would love it too, whatever it was, because she loved her father, adored him in fact. He seemed huge to her, a great bear of a man with sparkling brown eyes all full of life and joy and not a little mischief. Always making jokes, making her mother laugh, who did not laugh easily, her father was the happiest man in their village. Everyone said so, but Esther knew it to be true herself, even if no one said it. When he laughed, peels of thunder rolled down Mt. Hermon's shoulders, and he laughed a lot.

Esther loved to clamber onto his lap, climbing him like an ibex on a mountainside. She loved her mother. It was to her she turned for healing kisses on her girlish scratches. But her father was her private possession, her beast of burden, teller of tales, and the explainer of all the wonders of the earth.

An only child, she shared her pet reluctantly with others such as the village elders or even her mother. Esther knew she was the light of his life, and she reveled in the role. Beloved of her father, she strode through the world like the Jewish queen for whom she was named, surveying her subjects from the safe perch of his benevolent arms, serene in the confidence of a princess born to privilege.

"Show me!" Esther squealed. "Show me!"

"There, Esther. You see how he waves the

sheaf toward heaven. The first fruits are being lifted up to heaven as a wave offering. Do you see? Now listen."

The throng began to cheer and the sound was deafening, reverberating off the walls of the temple and the stone buildings around it. Bethphage, her village, was only a short walk from the temple, but to her tiny legs it seemed a great journey, an exciting trek to a faraway city where huge crowds could be seen and where wonderful sweets abounded. These her father enjoyed as much as Esther did, wolfing them down like a ravenous boy at a Bar Mitzvah, laughing at the sight of her bulging cheeks and pretending that he would eat her share after he finished his own.

On the way back to Bethphage that evening, her tummy full of almond cakes, she snuggled against her father's beard. Exhausted now from the feasting and the walking, allowing herself to be carried in his arms, she raked his beard and drifted toward the warm embrace of sleep. She knew she would be asleep before they crossed the Kidron.

"What does it mean, Abba?"

"First fruits? It is our gratitude for a new crop.

The first fruits are special."

"Like me?"

"Yes, Esther, like you."

"What else? Tell me more."

"There is more, but I'm not sure what all of it is." She smiled sleepily. She knew he was teasing her. He knew everything. "When Messiah comes, He will explain it all to us."

She heard no more. Asleep in the arms of her father she knew that she was his first fruit. Down, down into the Kidron Valley, he carried her, then up toward Bethphage and home. She dreamt of almond cakes, and he watched a secret smile steal across her lips.

"Messiah will come," he whispered. "He will make it all clear to both of us. For now, the feast is good enough."

*   *   *

Life is the history that precedes a death. Death is the history that comes before a resurrection. The resurrected life is born out of death, even as that same life was once born from the womb, and before that from the loins of two others. It is amazing that the resurrection scrapes at the rationalistic nerves of unbelievers. Amazing, because it is so in line with the rest of life's transitions.

A new life is created as one new body from two others. That new body then resides in fluid, a fish-like human, nine months in the waters of its primal baptism. If that baby were to breathe as it will one day breathe, it would die. The moment that human escapes its watery history, it dies to that historical state and can never go back to being able to live for more than a few moments under water. For nine months that new life, "buried" in water, develops into its birth form in liquid security, insulated against what lies ahead.

At birth that ends. Out into the blazing light and frigid cold of a stainless steel delivery room, a smack on the butt and a hearty scream, and the atmosphere is sucked into unused little lungs. From the warm comfort of a watery womb into a wider, harsher world, that tiny life must die to one place before it can burst kicking and *squalling* into another.

All of life is a chain of transitions. From a seed comes new life. From the womb comes the child. From the child, the adolescent, and from there to adulthood with any luck at all. The fruitful, productive adult grows elderly, a fading remnant of itself. The doorway of death leads to another realm and the form fit for that environment. Transition leads to transition, form giving way to form in the flow of life that leads to life.

The physical resurrection of Jesus of Nazareth was the statement of God that none of the walls of those transitions are barriers to Him. God is not trapped. He is no slave to order. From life to death, or from death to life, they are the same to Him. From word to flesh, from Mary's body into a putrid world, from His body into the throne room of the heavenlies and from the heavenlies to the Galilee—God orders the transitions; the transitions do not order God. That is the great truth of the resurrection. From God's presence into a body or from the body into His presence and back again, the grave was no more the final stage than was Mary's womb or Joseph's carpenter's shop.

The great good news of Christ's resurrection was not simply that He somehow beat the normal pattern and escaped the claws of corruption. The great news is that He showed the way for us who will follow. He was not an only child, but "the first born from the dead." By His resurrection we now find hope and cling less tenaciously to our bodies. Because we live in them, know nothing of life without them, the very thought of leaving our bodies behind to turn to dirt is a fearful thought. Yet Christ has shown the way. Death need not be the elevator shaft down into the grave. It can be the doorway up into yet another and far more glorious transition.

The grave has lost its sting. Death is swallowed up in victory.

*   *   *

The room was choked with dark confusion. These reports should have filled them all with joy, might well have in fact, except that they all came from the wrong people and all happened in the wrong places. What might well have been a moment of exhilarating anticipation had become an acidic argument.

Peter, never one for complex explanations, simply spread his huge hands palm-side up and shrugged his shoulders. "Am I a rabbi? How can I explain what I have not seen when I cannot even explain what I have seen?"

John, younger and more given to thought than the big fisherman, offered a simple fact, not an explanation, but a fact. "I only know what I saw. The tomb was empty." This brought a murmur from the others. "Peter went in. Ask him. Then there is what Mary told us. She said that He appeared to her and…"

The twin, who had said little in the three years of their journeys with Jesus, who had, in fact, been among *them* so quietly that he was easily overlooked, now brought his fist down hard on the table.

"I don't need Mary to tell me anything. I know what I saw. These two, also. He was there, I tell you. When He broke the bread our eyes were…"

"In Emmaus?" Andrew asked. "Why would He appear in Emmaus? For that matter, why would He appear to Mary at the tomb? None of this fits together. It's too many disconnected ends. I am a fisherman, like my brother. I can tell you, you cannot weave a net from broken threads."

The twin was resolute, his eyes firm, almost angry. "I know what I saw. I know who spoke to us. And you cannot talk me out of it."

"I'm not trying to talk you out of it. I just…"

Suddenly, Thomas stood up and raised his hand for silence. The abrupt and authoritative gesture was uncharacteristic of the thoughtful, cautious Thomas, and the room was instantly silent. Every eye was fixed on him.

"I speak only for myself. I'm not trying to persuade any of you of anything, but I have to say this. Think of what you are talking about. Resurrection from the dead? Think now. If you saw His ghost in Emmaus…"

"It wasn't His ghost. I'm telling you…"

"Please, let me finish. If it was Jesus in the flesh, if He is really resurrected, then logic says He must be raised in the same body."

"I'm not sure logic…"

"No. Listen to me. Logic says that body must have the marks of His crucifixion. If He is in a new body, then where is the old, the one we knew? No. If He is really alive, and I'm not saying I believe this, but if He is alive, would not the scars still be there?"

"I suppose so, but…"

"Well, then my position is clear. Unless I put my finger in the nail holes, I will not believe. Did you see that soldier thrust his spear in under Jesus' ribs? I want to put my hand in there. Then, and only then, will I believe."

No one could think of a response to this, not

even John. The brothers who claimed to have seen Him at the table in Emmaus grimaced and shook their heads, but they said nothing. What was there to say? Thomas had drawn a line, a hard line, and dared God to cross it. Nervously they shifted in their seats, uncertain whether to think Thomas bold or presumptuous.

At that very moment, without warning, light filled the room, not gradually, but all at once, bursting in upon them, banishing all darkness. Each man battled his own emotions, each different, but all in inner riot.

Then into the lighted room, through the wall, not parting it, not bursting it asunder, but passing through it, as through air, He stood before them. There was no doubt. This was not a look-alike or an illusion. No corporate fantasy had seized their imaginations. It was Jesus.

"Hail. *Shalom alaikum.*"

No one answered. No one even breathed.

He walked purposefully to Thomas. Jesus' eyes, with no hint of rebuke, were fixed on Thomas in that unwavering, piercing gaze that had unsettled publicans and enraged the Pharisees. Extending His hands, He spoke, not to the room, but to Thomas, into Thomas, slicing

43

through him like a blade.

"Behold, Thomas. Even as you have asked. Touch Me here. Do you see? Do it, Thomas. It is what you wanted, is it not? And here. My side. Put your hand in here. That's right."

Thomas dropped to his knees as though felled by a hammer.

"My Lord and my God."

CHAPTER 5

WHY NOT JUDAS?

L OVE IS a tapestry of resurrections, little deaths and small resurrections woven into a design of exquisite beauty. Each good-bye, every night spent apart from each other, lying alone in an empty bed, is a death. Reunions at airports, wild sweet kisses of great longing and joy like a fountain, are so sublime that the deaths they end are made the sweet sorrow necessary to know the sorrowful sweetness of shared resurrections.

The saying is "out of sight, out of mind." We are trapped by our senses, limited in our perception of reality by what we see and touch and taste. Memory may empower duty or reinforce hope, but a life remembered is a shadow. Children, the closer to infants they are, know all about it. Daddy is not "at work." "At work" is a grown-up illusion. The child only knows Daddy is gone, taken away, out of her sight. Daddy cannot hold the child though she knows he has held her. He is not at this moment tossing her in the air. He has and perhaps he will again, but the one is memory and the other hope.

With a shout of glee and a mad dash down the driveway, glorious resurrection ends the day of separation. Daddy's home! He is alive again, he who was buried in whatever "at work" means. The child's rejoicing, unfettered and unfeigned, is about new life, a relationship renewed and the delight that "at work" has been defeated yet again.

Let the dog bark! Get the bat and ball. The evening's feast will follow later. Mother will join them then, but now, right now in the driveway, the resurrection is personal. Daddy is not just *home*. He is home to her.

Every personal encounter with God is a resurrection experience. He meets us by the garden tomb, calls us by name as He did Mary, and drives away the death of separation. After a failure, after falling to the power of death within us, when we turn to Him for forgiveness, what we want is a resurrection, not ours, but His.

We ache to know that He is still alive, still knows our name, and still speaks the word of grace. What a tragedy when believers who have stumbled badly find only cold doctrinal comfort.

When we stand by the tomb and weep, it is not merely because He is dead, but because we were the cause.

What have I done?

Remorse is insufficient. My tears can never raise the Christ whose death my sins have wrought. Hysteria crowds in. Fear grips my guilty soul. What have I done? Have I gone too far this time? My sin has silenced a life of Sunday school lessons on the power of the blood. Doc-. trine cannot reach me now. Being dead in the shadowland of guilt, my despair bordering on hysteria, I need more. I must hear His voice.

*   *   *

The night of fishing had proven futile and, even worse, depressing. They had not a single fish to show for their efforts hauling wet nets all night. Now in the damp chill of dawn, conversation ceased. They had tried to keep some casual chatter going, even attempting some lame humor, but nothing amused Peter anymore. Without his booming laughter and rowdy jesting the conversation soon died until, at the first blush of morning, attempts at talk were as empty as their nets.

Peter, sullen and withdrawn, sat glumly in the

stern, his face in his hands. The others began to lean to the oars, but Peter gave no sign of helping. His pain-filled eyes bored holes in the bottom of their boat. Peter looked up only when a man's voice rang out across the lake.

"Have you caught much?"

"Nothing," John called back.

"Cast your net on the right side of the boat. Over there. Yes, yes, right there. That's where the fish are."

This brought some murmured discussion from the burly men in the boat. Who did this fellow think he was? Nobody can see where the schools are, at least not from the shore, at shouting distance from the boat. "Still," someone said, "what could it hurt to make one last cast?" They shrugged. What could it hurt?

They cast their net and began to draw first the tightening cord and then the net. Bulging with fish, the weight strained their backs as no haul they had ever taken. *No,* John thought, *that is not exactly true.* Once before, their friend had entered their boat and...

"Peter, it's Him! It's the Lord."

The big man shielded his eyes against the rising sun. Without a word he donned his shirt and plunged overboard. How like him, so impetuous and full of emotion. The others labored with the nets. Such bounty could not be wasted. Let Peter go on ahead. These fish had to be dealt with.

Dragging himself up out of the lake, Peter saw that it was indeed their friend. The dawn chill seeped into the marrow of his joints as lake water matted his thick, black hair and made his clothes a cold, wet anchor. Ahead of him, Jesus waited on the pebbled shore beside a charcoal fire. Fish spitted on sticks sizzled above the glowing coals, and great slabs of bread were toasting on a flat rock nestled amidst the embers. Behind these, squatting by the fire like a common cook, was the Lord Himself.

Peter stood shivering, not from the chill alone, but from the aching guilt that threatened to swallow him whole. Jesus' eyes, brown and deep, eternal eyes that cut right through a man, those eyes were fixed on Peter's face. Dread and hope warred within the fisherman. What would his friend say now? Certainly Peter deserved stern words of rebuke from his friend. Perhaps their friendship was ended. That also would be deserved. What rejection had Peter not earned for himself? What punishment should he be spared? What eternal damnation?

Peter waited. He had no idea what to say. No apology could be sufficient for his cowardice and betrayal. Judas had hanged himself. Peter could not even manage that. Fear, guilt, and shame bound his tongue. He must let Jesus speak first, must let Him make whatever lashing rebuke was called for. At least the others were not here to hear it. Peter waited in anguish for the hot lava-flow of anger to spew out upon him. He had no defense, not even an explanation for what he had done. In the air between them hung Peter's denial that night in Caiaphas' courtyard. What could either of them say to break the spell of gloom that lay upon the moment?

Peter involuntarily extended his wet, cold fingers toward the glowing coals, and, keeping his eyes fixed on Jesus' face, he waited to see what his friend would say. Suddenly, the moment became a reenactment of the horrible night, a recreation of his craven denial when he warmed his hands at a fire just like this one. That night in Caiaphas' courtyard he had met the Master's *gaze* just as he did now.

What *could* Jesus say? I saw you? I heard you? I know what you did? Peter ached for healing, not rebuke. Could it ever be the same again? Could he ever again eat with his friend without bitterness for bread and shame for sop?

Tenderness, like dawn upon the Golan Heights, cast a soft light on Jesus' eyes, and a secret smile toyed with the corners of His mouth. For one wild, delirious moment, Peter thought his friend was about to wink. Instead, he spoke, and in His voice Peter heard no trace of rancor.

"Come and dine."

*   *   *

There are only two places in all of the New Testament where a "charcoal fire" is described in just those words. One is the one on which Jesus cooked and to which He welcomed His dripping, wounded friend. The other, the first, was in Caiaphas' courtyard, at which Peter warmed his hands. There, identified as a Galilean and a friend of Jesus, Peter cursed and denied the man who had prophesied that he would do so.

Perhaps Jesus prepared just such a fire, recreated a place of painful remembrance where Peter could be healed of his most crippling memory. Two of the postresurrection appearances of Jesus are at table. With a meal, Jesus offered comfort at Emmaus and grace in Galilee. His resurrection meant personal fellowship, renewal of relationship, and a new life free of guilt and condemnation.

When, in our moments of deepest loneliness, we turn to Christ, our comfort is not in the doctrine of the resurrection but in His fellowship with us. That is the message of Emmaus. He listens and explains. He walks with us, breaks bread with us, and comforts us with words of revelation.

In Galilee it was different. Peter was not looking for understanding. The kind of biblical instruction Jesus gave on the road to Emmaus would have meant little to Peter on that chilly dawn. Peter was not looking for Old Covenant insight on the crucifixion of Messiah. He longed for New Covenant grace granted by a risen Lord.

Jesus did not ignore Peter's sinful denial. He met him in the place of pain, re-created the setting, and summoned Peter back there. Alive again, not separate from Peter's remorse, but alive within it, Jesus rose not just *for* Peter, but *to* Peter. The resurrection of Jesus Christ was personal, had to be personal, had to mean healing and forgiveness for Simon Peter, or it meant nothing for humanity at large.

The resurrection of Christ was, of course, for all humanity. Its announcement, however, its human expression, was up close and personal, to individuals, not to the masses. To Mary first, then to the chaps on the road to Emmaus, and at last to Peter on the rocky beach of Lake Gennesaret, Jesus rose to individuals. These isolated appearances speak to the very point of the resurrection. Mary was the point. Peter was the point. Renewed fellowship with the wounded and fallen, fellowship with french fries on the side is the very personal point of Christ's resurrection.

Christ's resurrection is not for *us*, but for *me*. He rises to walk with me, to explain the purpose of suffering over broken bread. He calls me by name. It is not *our* sins He forgives, and certainly not *theirs*, never *theirs*. He forgives *me*. He meets me on the beach and beckons me to His fireside. He invites me to take communion, feeds *me* on His flesh, and lifts His cup to *my* lips. Come and dine, I hear him say, but not to *them*. He speaks to me.

What made the difference for Simon Peter? In many respects he had treated Jesus no better than Judas did. Judas denied Christ for money. Peter did the same for cowardice. Judas lusted for gold. Peter's passion was to save his hide. Peter had been closer to Jesus than Judas and, unlike Judas, had loudly rejected Christ's prophecy of denial, promising to follow his friend to the cross. Likewise a case can be made that Judas' remorse was at least as broken-hearted as Peter's. Peter wept. Judas hanged himself. Suicide may be over-the-top, unbalanced grief, but it hardly speaks of a cavalier spirit.

Yet it was Peter who recovered, who became the founding patriarch, who went on to live in Pentecostal power and to die for his Lord. The world knows their names, Judas the betrayer and Peter the saint.

One must wonder, what if Judas had just waited? Mightn't he have encountered the resurrected Lord, heard words of grace and healing, and even resumed his place among the twelve? We will never know, of course, but Peter's blessed encounter with Jesus in Galilee gives us room to wonder what might have been if Judas had only waited.

The spiritual deathblow for Judas was not his materialistic betrayal of the Son of God, though that was sin enough. It was not even the heinous artifice of his kiss in Gethsemane. What sealed the damnation of Judas was that he cut himself off from the resurrection. Was Judas' betrayal "unforgivable"? Perhaps, but Jesus forgave much that was unforgivable. He forgave those who slew Him and those that mocked Him as He died. He forgave Peter for cowardice, Paul for murder, and a pitiful, unnamed woman for adultery.

Have the sins of your past slain all your hope of holiness? The resurrection is real. Does death reign in your life and relationships? The resurrection is real. You may think you have gone too far, sinned too horribly, done the unforgivable. None of what you have done can negate what He has done. You may think your sin an immovable boulder. He has rolled the stone away. You may be all alone, right now, even as you read this, alone in a place of death. Look up. Lift up your eyes. Listen. He calls your name; not humanity, but *your* name. There, just there. Do you see Him? Arms outstretched He waits beside a charcoal fire. He waits for you. Do you fear His words of rebuke, His scowling, scolding rejection? You may think all is spoiled, never to be the same. Listen! He speaks to you.

RESURRECTION

"Come and dine. Sit here, My child, and tell Me all about it. What things? Eat. Live, for I am alive."

What a tragic irony that liberal theologians should fall to the Judas error, not the denial of Christ, but the denial of His resurrection. Those who blithely reject the bodily resurrection of Jesus cut themselves off from its benefit. They reduce the resurrection to an idea, a "corporate wish." Hoping to demythologize Christianity, they eviscerate their own hope. There is no power to raise us in a Christ who was not raised. If Jesus was not raised, physically raised from the dead, Christianity is a fool's parade. If He was raised, and He was, those who deny the resurrection, those who water it down with the condescending language of "myth," are become fools, not because of Peter's sin but by the sin of Judas.

The resurrection of Christ is not optional theological equipment. The empty tomb is the foundation of our faith, the great truth and the eternal hope. If Jesus died a martyr's death, a good example executed by envious bad examples, if that was the end of it, then we are doomed. If the grave conquered Him, then the grave is our end as well. If the resurrection is nothing but a shared wish, we face a shared abyss. Liberal theologians, so called, rummage about among intellectual gravestones looking for fresh ways to express their lethal unbelief.

The moralist, the humanistic do-gooder and the raucous Hollywood icon search in one cause célèbre after another hoping for hope. They think they will find Jesus, *some* Jesus, *any* Jesus, one they approve of anyway, among their cobbled-together religions, false spirituality, and New Age nonsense.

> Why seek ye the living among the dead?
> He is not here, but is risen...
> —LUKE 24:5–6

Magic crystals, channeled ancestors, and weird theological perversions are the stuff of death. The one great hope is the empty tomb. Simple, mysterious, scandalous, and majestic, the factual, physical resurrection, just as the Bible reports it, is the truth, the only truth, that mocks the grave and does death to death.

Christ is risen. He is risen indeed!

CHAPTER 6

THE CULTURE OF DEATH

S HE REBUKED him with her eyes. Her voice was cold accusation, and her words were nails thrown one at a time into a metal pan.

"Why didn't You come? My brother would not have died if only You had gotten here on time. He was Your friend. You know that he loved You. Why didn't You come?"

Peering from under her head covering she regarded Him darkly. The gathering crowd watched the scene with morbid fascination. Would she rail on Him? Would He defend Himself? Even for a man as beloved as Lazarus, sufficient days of mourning had been accomplished, not by paid mourners as was often the case, but by a host of genuinely grieving friends and relatives. Hanging over the funeral had been one question. Why didn't Jesus come? Lazarus had been Jesus' official host and generous sponsor. Whenever the Teacher came to Bethany or Bethphage or even Jerusalem, it was His custom to lodge with Lazarus and his sisters. They could see the hurt in Martha's eyes, and no one blamed her. Jesus could have gotten here, *should* have, in fact. She was right to treat Him coldly. What they wanted to know, to see with their own eyes, was what Jesus would do.

His eyes brimming with unfeigned tears, and in His voice no hint of anger or self-defense, He melted her chilly reserve. He did love her brother. She knew that, could see that in His tears. He loved her as well. His tears were not just tears of grief for a dead friend, but tears of compassion for a grieving woman. How could she stay angry with Him? After all, her brother's death was not really His fault. People die. If Jesus had gotten here earlier, He might well have healed Lazarus. Perhaps only God could know such things. What she did know was that it was too late now. Healing the sick is one thing, but raising the dead is another. She was surprised, however, when Jesus, as though He could hear her thoughts, asked her view on the resurrection.

"Do you believe your brother will rise?"

"I know he will rise, as we all will."

Was He testing her? Was she a rabbi to be asked such things? Or a Sadducee to deny the resurrection? Messiah would raise the dead. She had been told that from her girlhood. Her brother had often joked how lucky they were to live where they did. Since the prophets said Messiah would first raise those buried on the Mount of Olives, to own a tomb there was a good thing. Of course, she believed in the resurrection. She expanded her answer with what she hoped sounded like emphatic faith.

"My brother will rise in the resurrection." His response stunned her and sent a wave of murmuring back through the throng of onlookers.

"I am the resurrection."

*　　*　　*

Jesus Himself, that is the greatest truth of all. Neither His deeds, nor His blessings, nor words spoken of Him are the great Truth. He *is* the Way, the Truth, and the Life. He is also the resurrection. It is not just that someday Messiah will raise the dead, though that would be hope enough. The great *truth*, the magnificent *truth* is that in Him we are already raised. The secret of the gospel is the *truth* of Him in the truth of us, His life in our life. In Him we are already raised to newness of life, fullness of life, and abundance of life. There is a great resurrection to come, but its power is already at work in us.

Death has lost its fearsomeness because we are already raised beyond its reach. We will live because we already do. We will be raised because we already are raised. As death was once at work in us, so now the resurrection is at work in us.

Paul said, "For to me to live is Christ, and to die is gain" (Phil. 1:21).

That is true, and it is true because of the resurrection. He is raised in me and I in him. His life is revealed now in terms of me. My glorified body is yet to be mine, but the resurrection that will make it mine is already mine.

> I am crucified with Christ: nevertheless I live; yet not I, but Christ...who loved me, and gave himself for me.
> —GALATIANS 2:20

That means that His resurrection power is already at work in all of my life. The power of the resurrection is at work in marriage to raise it up to new life. In the intellect, in creativity, in relationships, and even in business, the power of His resurrection is at work within us. Behind bars His resurrection power sets prisoners free.

RESURRECTION

In bars His resurrection breaks the chains of alcoholism. His resurrection is more powerful than the death of cocaine, the prison house of lust, and the grave of hateful unforgiveness.

To cut oneself off, as Judas did, from the power of that resurrection is to obviate the effect of Christ's finished work. The blood is on the mercy seat *because* He rose. The covenant of grace is in effect *because* He rose. We may access the commonwealth of sonship *because* He rose.

Judas would not wait. Having murdered Truth, Life, and Hope, he murdered himself. We live in a Judas world, a culture obsessed with abortions. We abort babies, marriages, and lives in a mad celebration of death. We even ceremonialize it. Some churches now have divorce ceremonies to mark the abortion of marriages, and women who have aborted babies are held up as suffering heroes.

Perhaps the day is fast approaching when postmoderns will read the New Testament and see Judas as the hero. Why not? He acted boldly, refusing to knuckle under to such prosaic conventions as loyalty. He managed to find personal advantage, even profit in what was obviously an inevitable tragedy. Then, at last, absorbed with his own emotion, he yielded to the culture of death, nobly choosing to abort himself rather than live on in a quality of life sadly lessened by pain. Why, he is perfect.

Yet it is those who wait in faith, those who welcome Christ's resurrection into their remorse and pain who find His power. He is the resurrection and the life, not just in concept but in dead marriages. The couple who chooses to embrace with faith the possibilities of an infirm child rather than end his little life in the womb is in a place to experience Christ's resurrection power. The couple that struggles through and resists the popular impulse to walk off and leave their marriage in the tomb, that couple is in a place to know His resurrection power. In the current culture of death, the power of the resurrection is the message of the hour.

Postmodern culture loves a winner, and to the unredeemed, death looks like a true champion. Our society enshrines death, writes poetry to its glory, and hurls the wounded, the weak, and the defenseless into its cruel arms as a sacrifice. Suicide, abortion, and euthanasia throw sacrifices to the postmodern Molech while society dances the dance of death.

RESURRECTION

Yet into those graveyard that welcome Him, Jesus comes with power, not offended by our grief, but comforting us with His own tears. He lifts us beyond our pain and banishes death with a word.

*　　*　　*

The afternoon heat in the cemetery was staggering, a stupefying furnace that had driven the inhabitants of Bethany indoors for naps. The wildflowers of spring were long-forgotten memories of splendid color, and in their place the rocky ground wore only a thread-bare shawl of thirsty, brown grass. At the edge of the graveyard, cropping without enthusiasm, several goats meandered aimlessly among the rocks. Their guardian, a small, brown boy with rebellious black curls and skinny legs, dozed in a tiny patch of shade afforded by an ancient fig tree. Bare arms resting on his knobby knees supported the shaggy head in a dreamless, heat-battered sleep. The goats were not going anywhere.

Noise, the rapidly growing sound of voices, lots of voices, pierced the silence and snapped the lad's head up. Whether at his sudden motion or because they heard the disturbance at the same moment, the animals started, moving a few steps further toward the jagged hillside and away from the graves and tombs.

The boy, Enoch by name, watched a throng of noisy adults from the village spill in through the open gate of the rock wall surrounding the upper face of the cave-pocked graveyard. This was unusual indeed. It was obviously not a funeral, but what it was he could not tell. Enoch determined to get closer. There might be something here worth seeing, something, at least, to break the tedium.

It became apparent that at the center of the storm was a man whom he did not recognize. Enoch did not know the name of all the adults in Bethany, of course, but this man did not live in the village. Enoch was certain of that. The stranger Himself was silent, but every word of the others seemed to be directed at Him. Some called out to Him from the crowd not angrily, but urgently. Fighting to get close enough to hear and see, Enoch wormed his way through the legs of the adults, some of whom kicked at him. He took no great offense. He was used to being kicked at.

At last he could see the man clearly. Oddly

enough, the man looked surprisingly like Enoch's father, only He was sober and His eyes showed no hint of dark rage. The stranger was of average height, barrel-chested, and had firm muscular arms and the hands of a working man.

His face was craggy and not at all handsome, with a large nose that hooked too sharply to be attractive. His voice, when He spoke, was strong and full of authority but held no hint of anger.

"Where have you laid him?"

Enoch recognized the woman who answered, but he did not know her name. She was the sister, one of them at least, of Lazarus, the man who had recently died. The shepherd boy knew Lazarus, as did all the children. A strange household indeed were Lazarus and his sisters. All three were spinsters, too large, too unattractive, and too old to ever marry. Lazarus was prosperous, very prosperous, and as generous as he was successful. Having no children of his own, Lazarus spoiled the children of others, especially the poor children of notorious drunkards. Enoch would miss him.

The sisters of Lazarus bore an unfortunate resemblance to their brother, overly tall for women, large-boned and horse-faced. One was as kind and generous as her brother. The other did not approve of Lazarus' eccentric affection for village waifs and shooed them away from her house whenever Lazarus was not there to stop her. It was clear to Enoch that often the wrong adults die.

"There, Master. My brother is there in that tomb. The second from the end."

"Roll away the stone," the stranger said, and a shocked murmur rose from the onlookers.

"No, Master, no!" a woman protested, and Enoch recognized her as the colder and less generous sister. "He has been dead four days. The odor will be horrible."

Enoch squeezed through the crowd. He must get closer. This was getting interesting. He could see the stranger's face more clearly now. Up close He was even less attractive than Enoch had thought. Perhaps He and Lazarus' homely sisters were related.

It was apparent, even to Enoch, that this man was in charge, but not because He screamed or slapped anyone as Enoch's father would certainly have done. This man simply did not argue with the woman. He merely repeated His command with no change of tone, as though the woman had not spoken, as though no argument, no objection could possibly be offered that had any weight whatsoever.

Indeed, no one said anything else. The woman, Lazarus' sister, gave only the slightest nod, and three young men scurried to the massive stone disk to roll it along the trough and away from the cave's mouth. Enoch saw several women cover their faces with the headscarves, but no sound, not a single word pierced the silence. Even Enoch's goats stood still.

The stranger took two or three steps toward the open tomb and raised His hand. His back to Enoch and the others, His rich, deep voice rang out in the silence. The sound of it was firm, but not particularly loud, and the words were clear and simple.

"Lazarus, come forth."

Not a sound, not even a bird song. Silence. Enoch had never felt anything like it. The skin on his smooth brown arms prickled in goose flesh, and he found it hard to breathe. His eyes were fixed on the gaping mouth of the tomb.

A sudden movement, a flash of white from inside the cave made the crowd gasp. Bending low at the entrance then straightened to his full height, a man stepped out still wrapped tightly in grave clothes. A woman behind Enoch screamed. He heard movement at the edge of the crowd behind him, the sound of feet running. Who could move? How could anyone run away? Why would they?

At last the stranger spoke again, His calm, masculine voice showing no hint of surprise or even excitement. His words, just as before, were simple and impossible to misunderstand. Enoch knew that if he lived to be an old man he would never forget them.

"Unbind him and let him go."

*   *   *

It is Christ's resurrection power that calls forth the dead to newness of life. The same power that worked in Christ's dead body to bring it alive from the grip of the grave now works in us to grant new life. Romans chapter 1 identifies a connection between three great truths: holiness, resurrection, and grace.

> Jesus...was...declared to be the Son of God with power, according to the spirit of holiness by the resurrection from

the dead: By whom we have received grace...

—ROMANS 1:3–5

In other words the Holy Spirit, that very power that raised Christ's body, is the Spirit of grace. Therefore, as Christ was raised by the Spirit of holiness, that same Spirit now grants us the grace to live free, happy, holy lives. Christians are not, as some bumper stickers suggest, merely forgiven sinners. As Christ Himself was the "first born from the dead," we, His handiwork, are likewise raised from the dead. Jesus was the first to be followed by many. An abundant harvest always follows the first fruits.

Paul put it this way: "Therefore we are buried with him by baptism into death: that like as Christ was raised up from the dead by the glory of the Father, even so we also should walk in newness of life" *(Rom. 6:4). The witness of the saints is not to forgiveness alone. Ours is the testimony of Lazarus. Can you hear his voice in the synagogue on the Sabbath after his resurrection? What did he say? My sins are forgiven? If he spoke of forgiveness at all, it was not of that alone.*

"I was dead," he surely said, "and stank in my decay." Then his voice ripped the inky doom like

70

a sword. "He called my name. Power flooded my corpse, and holy breath rushed in to fill my lungs with life. Look on me and believe. I once was dead, but now I live. By the power of the Spirit of grace His resurrection is mine."

Was the Lazarus who walked out of the grave the same man who was carried in? Certainly not! Proof of that is Lazarus' name being added by Jesus' enemies to their hit list. Those who sought to slay Jesus wanted to kill Lazarus as well. Why? The resurrection! The hatred of hell is fixed on those who now live, not just as forgiven sinners, but as living proof of the resurrection.

PART 2

ON RAISING THE DEAD

CHAPTER 7

LIFE AND DEATH
IN THE LAND OF SPAMALOT

Monty Python's memorable scene of
the death wagon, like so many of their
vignettes, is flush with terrifying, side-splitting
truth. It goes like this for those who have not
ventured into the land of Spamalot.

Through the muddy streets of a medieval city
under siege, a wagon of corpses is being dragged
by a bored attendant who drones a gruesome
chant:

> Bring out your dead,
> Bring out your dead.

A man carrying his elderly father over his
shoulder approaches the wagon and attempts
to off-load the body. Before he can, the "corpse"
lifts his head and announces that he is "not dead
yet." After some debate and negotiation they
brain the old man with a club and throw him on
the cart of corpses.

Western culture has begun a nightmare

journey into the land of Spamalot. The near dead are despised, their protests and the protests of those who care are ignored, before we bash out their brains, not with clubs, but with judges. The elderly are not safe in Spamalot. Neither are the unborn, the half-born, the infirm, and the mentally impaired. The land of Spamalot is dangerous, in fact, to everyone except those who wield the club.

We are too quick to toss the barely alive on the wagon of death. Oddly enough, those who talk the most about the value of life, who plead, as they should, for the weak and unborn, are often the first to toss the sin-bound on the death cart. They weep for tiny corpses carried out with the trash at the back doors of abortion mills, but they will not lift a finger to raise a crack-addicted and pregnant prostitute from the dust of death.

We somehow seem to find boundless energy to squabble inside the church, but we cannot rouse ourselves to revive those dying outside in the street. We have turned Jesus' directive top-side down. We raise the devil and cast out the dead. The land of Spamalot is not safe enough for the weak, and the church of Spamalot is not powerful enough for the dead.

RESURRECTION

A homosexual, inflamed with perverse lust and in bondage to his appetites, finds no help from either the "liberals" or the "fundamentalists" in Spamalot. The liberals tell him his sins are an alternative lifestyle and thereby cut him off from grace, because the grace of forgiveness is only for the sinful. Angry fundamentalists are hardly of more help because they despise homosexuals, shunning them as untouchables with infectious diseases.

Both are wrong. He has neither an alternative sexual orientation nor an infectious disease. He is dead in his sins. Teaching him to "accept himself" as a homosexual will damn him, and hating him has none of the power of life. Only a resurrection will do, and only a resurrected church is the instrument of power.

For all the dead, not just for the nice dead but for the nasty dead as well, the hope, the only hope, is resurrection. The drug addict and power addict both need life. The meth-fueled solo robber and the conspiracy of pirate accountants suffer the same condition. They are dead. A rich thief is no more alive then a poor one. Death in the penthouse is no nearer life than death in the gutter. Death is death, and there is no medicine for death. The dead cannot be counseled out of their graves, and "affirming" them in their death is but to toss them on the cart.

This poor, staggering, death-obsessed post-modern culture of ours is longing for a voice crying in the streets.

Bring out your dead.

A church fully alive in resurrection power must find its voice.

Bring out your dead.

When they carry their corpses out to us we dare not load them on a death cart or bludgeon those who die too slowly to please us. We need a new paradigm of ministry for the new era. In fact, we need one so old that it is new.

"Bring out your dead," we must cry, "that they may live again."

Postmodern culture, spiritually confused, ego-centric, doubting ultimate truth, and drunk on entertainment, will tax the creativity and anointing of the church as has no age since ancient Rome. In most places believers are not yet thrown to the lions, but that may not be all that far off. One television comedian, to great laughter, by the way, read his list of candidates for death in the Iraq war instead of those brave soldiers serving there. Among them was a successful actor whose only offense seemed to be that he had recently announced he was a Christian. The return of the blood-soaked coliseum may not be as faraway as we would like to believe.

If the response of a turtlesque church is to pull in its head at the rolling thunder, the greatest opportunity for revival in two thousand years will be missed. This is hardly the time for fortress building. It is the day to deny fear its victory and to stretch out in ministry, a ministry emboldened by faith, motivated by loving compassion, and empowered by Christ's resurrection.

In 2 Kings, the fourth chapter, there is an account of Elisha raising a dead boy. In this rich story of resurrection there are powerful insights for ministry in the twenty-first century. In the face of this postmodern era, or perhaps we should say post-Christian era, new models of ministry must be found or the church will continue to limp into irrelevancy. The church, in the West, at least, is in danger of becoming a quaint antique, marginalized and ceremonial, unable to touch contemporary culture with transforming power. For that, a resurrection model is needed. The miracle and the mystery

of *the Resurrection* and of the several other resurrections in Scripture can be translated into a
new working model that raises ministry itself
from death to new life. A dead organization
afraid of its own market is hardly an instrument
of mysterious resurrection power.

Elisha shows the way. The resurrection is not
dead doctrine, but the ministry of transforming life. In this needy age we can entertain the
saints and build sanctuaries against the world,
or we can enter boldly as Elisha did and raise
the dead.

*   *   *

Shielding his eyes against the blazing sun, the
prophet squinted down from his hilltop retreat.
A frail stream cut a jagged scar across the pale
green belly of the valley below. From the far
side, across the rustic, stone bridge, two people
pressed forward at an impressive pace straight
toward where he stood.

A man, a working type, led a saddled ass rid-
den by a woman. His eyes were on the bridge,
but the woman peered up toward the prophet,
trying to pick him out among the trees. The
beast lurched a bit as it stepped from the bridge,

and her head covering fell away. That is when the prophet recognized her and spoke to his assistant.

"Look down there. It's that Shunammite woman. You remember, the one to whom God gave a son. Go and meet her. Ask if all in her house are well, she and the husband and the boy. That child must be, what, six or seven now. Go meet her."

With growing concern the prophet watched the encounter below between his assistant and the Shunammite woman. Her features were tight, obviously strained, but by no means hysterical. Gehazi, his assistant, spoke softly, so softly that the prophet could not hear his words. The woman, however, despite her ashen appearance spoke firmly, not shouting, but with a strong confidence that belied her grave countenance.

"It is well," she announced.

Gehazi began to further argue with the woman when her eyes fell on Elisha. Rushing past the stammering Gehazi, she plunged headlong at the prophet's feet; clutching him by the ankles she began not so much to plead as to rebuke the great man of God. The prophet of Carmel who made kings to tremble obviously terrified this humble woman of Shunem not at all. She lay, her face in the dirt, humbly clutching the prophet's ankles, but her tone was decidedly accusatory.

"I never asked you for a son, did I? Did I come to you and plead for a son? You cannot just walk into a poor woman's life and give her a child only to let that child die. Prophet or no prophet, that is not right."

＊   ＊   ＊

The real hero in the resurrection of the dead boy in 2 Kings 4 is not Elisha. It is surely not Gehazi, that loser. The heroes are two, an unnamed woman of great faith and a God who was on the scene before Elisha showed up. This Shunammite woman, faced with death, was moved by bold faith into a personal encounter with resurrection ministry.

There is no place of need into which Christian ministry can reach that is not already being bombarded by someone's prayer of faith. Before the evangelist preaches or the soulwinner knocks on the door, someone's grandmother is praying. When the church invades a drug-infested urban area, someone on the inside is already refusing to accept the grip of death. Elisha may land the

81

troops, but it is the Shunammite hero, the person of resurrection faith, who shells the shore.

Global Servants, which I head, and Mountain Foreign Missions (MFM) cooperated to build a Bible school in Mexico. The buildings were finally built, and the dedication ceremony was scheduled for the next day when Helen Mann (then president of MFM) and I, along with five other Americans and three Mexicans, toured the sight. We were informed, to our dismay, that the well had dried up, absolutely *dried up*, and after all the well company could do, no water was to be found anywhere on the property. It was a disaster!

The entire group gathered around the well, and, joining hands, we prayed ferociously in what we thought was faith. In certain circles volume counts for faith and sweat for anointing. Helen would have none of it. She chided us and then turned on God.

"That is the worst excuse for praying I've ever heard! Stop. Get back." Stepping to the edge of the well and looking at the sky she said, "Look at this. What do You have to say to this?"

With that she spun on her heal and marched off to the van, announcing that what we all needed was Mexican food and a good night's sleep. The well she had flung into God's lap, and she never gave it another thought.

The next morning the well was full, of course, and those of us on that trip learned what Elisha knew. God is moved by the prayers of old ladies and may actually be intimidated. Ministries that intend to raise the dead in this new era must know that the initiative was never theirs. Passionate intercessors moved by the heart of God in turn move the heart of God. Prayer and prevenient grace work hand in hand. The Shunammite woman and a God of resurrection power are on the job long before an Elisha shows up.

Prevenient grace is "grace that goes before." From the old English usage of *prevent*, which meant to "get there first," prevenient grace is operative when we are unaware of it, are not yet involved, and may not even want it. Any missionary worth her salt knows she is not taking God to Africa. God is in Africa waiting for her to show up.

It was a God of prevenient grace who moved on the Shunammite's heart to bestow resurrection faith, who caused Elisha to go with her, and it was God who waited in the room with the dead boy until the man of God arrived. Every resurrection is God's idea. There is no crack house, no den of the dead, where God is not and to which God is not summoning His church in resurrection power.

*   *   *

Thrusting Gehazi and the woman out, Elisha closed the door behind them and turned to the small body on the bed. Elisha had not asked the boy's age. What difference could that make now? Thin legs and arms flat against the bed, eyes closed by his mother's trembling fingers, the lad's face was waxen under a mask of death. Elisha had noticed before how much smaller bodies seemed in death.

Then it came upon him, that sense, that holy sense, not the voice, for that he had heard also, but an inner knowing. This sense was a mystery to be sure, but when it moved within him, when he listened and obeyed, it had never failed him. It was God. He knew that. But it was God inside. Elisha had heard the voice of God, the audible voice was from the outside. This was the inner nudge of God, a soft prod on the wall of his heart, but it was no less God than if He had spoken from the clouds. The problem was that the "nudge" was toward something he had never done or even seen. Against the law at worst and, at best, unconventional and eccentric, the thing was best done alone. Elisha was glad the boy's mother and Gehazi were not watching.

Climbing on the bed Elisha awkwardly straddled the dead child. He knew *what* he was supposed to do. It was the *how* that was proving difficult. On his hands and knees above the boy's corpse, Elisha hesitated only a second, then stretched himself full length on the body of death. Now face to face, mouth to mouth with the dead boy, Elisha let his weight down on the boy who felt even smaller under him than he had appeared.

Prayer like a spring burbled up within the great prophet and became a fountain of power. Beyond words, past cognition, life began to flow out of Elisha and into the dead boy. The prophet made no petition, would not, in fact, have known exactly what to ask for. He knew what was to happen, and prayer within him became the release of himself into that knowledge, into that reality, as the effluence of life drained him, emptying him as never before. Suddenly, without warning, the boy sneezed. He did not open his eyes. He just sneezed, softly, a child's hiccup of a sneeze, then sneezed again. Elisha lifted himself up on his hands and knees and stared intently into the boy's face. After a few seconds, the child sneezed again, then again and again, seven times in all, with growing intensity, but he was like someone talking in his sleep. When the sneezes stopped, the boy lay still, breathing now, but not fully awake. Neither dead nor alive, but in some state of half-life the boy had risen beyond the grip of death only to be seized by sleep like death.

Elisha dragged himself from the bed in near exhaustion and began to pace the room. The "sense" returned, stronger this time. The "sense of life," unstoppable and powerful, surged back into Elisha like wind into slack sails. Then prayer commingled with the "sense of life" to become one thing, one force within the prophet. Life and prayer in resurrection power became one stream into which Elisha hurled himself without reservation. As never before, Elisha knew that "sense" had become life within him.

Again stretching himself upon the sleeping child he prayed in full release, as before, not seeking, but surrendering. Instantly the power began its flow again. Warmth rushed back into the child's beardless cheeks, and his eyelashes fluttered. With a moan as soft as a sigh, the brown eyes popped open and stared into Elisha's. The prophet smiled but said nothing. Strangely enough, neither did the boy. Elisha wondered of how much of the day's struggle the boy was aware. What did he know? How much would he remember? Can the living remember death? The boy just blinked at Elisha as expressionless as a little brown-eyed owl.

Standing beside the bed, Elisha turned to the still-closed door and called for his assistant. The prophet was suddenly very tired, "Gehazi, call his mother. Tell her to come and fetch her son. He's in my bed, and I am weary."

CHAPTER 8

LIFE OR LAW

W HAT ELISHA did was against the law. That is to say, touching the corpse of that boy made Elisha unclean. If we are to raise the dead in the twenty-first century, we cannot be afraid of the dead. How can we be the salt of the earth if we are afraid of touching the dirt? Among the most beloved verses of evangelicals is 1 John 4:4, "Greater is he that is in you, than he that is in the world." Yet we act as though the danger of the world to corrupt us is greater than God's power through us to sanctify the world. If, in an effort to remain unspotted by the world, we allow the world to remain untouched by us, the dead will not be raised.

There is a balance to be sure. In order to raise the boy, Elisha did not have to die. A dead church cannot raise the dead, and the answer to a post-Christian world is certainly not a post-Christian church. We are beguiled if we think we must compromise the life within us in order to overcome death in the world. On the other hand, a sanctified, fully alive church has nothing to fear from touching the dead.

While speaking at a ministers' conference I met a Jewish car salesman in the lobby of the hotel. I was surprised by how intrigued he was with me and my friends. Soon his interest in us jelled into naked curiosity about our faith. In no time, his honest questions became a staircase that he climbed, one step after the other, right up to the very point of entry. It was obvious that for all his colorful language and pretended cynicism, this Jewish businessman was on the verge of accepting Christ. He must have sensed this himself, because at the last minute he made one desperate dash for the safety of the bar, declaring himself suddenly unspeakably thirsty.

"Well, this has been fascinating, but I need a drink. I'm sure you gents will excuse me."

"Let me come with you," I said. "You don't mind, do you? We can talk in a bar as well as we can out here."

"Well, I suppose," he agreed, with some obvious amusement.

I started into the bar with him when one of the ministers with me panicked and seized my arm. "Dr. Rutland, please. Think of your ministry."

"I am," I responded, trying to sound as comforting as I could. "It's in that bar."

Harold, which proved to be the salesman's name, drank two cocktails while he and I talked about Jesus of Nazareth. I, by the way, drank a diet soda. Neither of us seemed inclined to assail the other's choice of beverages, and the conversation drifted amiably toward a divine encounter between a Jewish car salesman and a Jewish carpenter.

After about an hour, Harold made an astounding observation. "If what you say is true, I have spent my entire life asking the wrong question. I've been asking what a Jew like me had to do with the Christ of the Christians. But that is not the question, is it? The real question is, how did a Gentile like you find faith in the Messiah of the Jews?"

"Harold," I said, "You are right at the threshold. Would you like to come on in?"

At that he made an astonishing physical response. To this day I am not sure of its full implications. He plucked the cocktail napkin from under his drink, laid it meticulously on the glass, and pushed it to the side. Then without a tear in his eye, as calmly as you please, he simply asked the way.

"What do I do?"

There in a smoke-filled hotel bar, a Jewish car salesman held my hand across a table stained with alcohol and prayed through to faith in Jesus. Six months later, Harold was an usher at one of the largest churches in the South.

We will never raise the dead if we are afraid to go into cemeteries. Anyway, why should we be? The dead cannot harm us. We do not have to be dead or even look dead to reach them. Some, with good motives I believe, are confused on that point. I do not have to dress like a pimp to lead one to Christ, or drink to reach a drunk, or even look young to reach the youthful. In fact, conforming long enough may have results I cannot afford in my life or my ministry. But it is not necessary. By the same token, neither is fear.

I was preaching in a holiness church on a Sunday morning when a late-arriving visitor entered. From where I was on the platform I could see this boy had no idea what he was supposed to do. His baggy trousers, clinging desperately to his lower hips, pooled luxuriously at the cuffs around bright red high-tops. His spiked hair, festive in its rainbow hues, pointed skyward in every direction.

RESURRECTION

The place was packed, and no obvious place to sit presented itself to his worried eyes. Likewise, none of the ushers hurried to help him. My heart sank when an elderly woman started toward him with a determined look on her face. She was a somber study in contrast to his unrestrained celebration of modernity. The considerable plushness of her grandmotherly form was swathed in a black dress that covered her from calf to wrist. Her face, which bore no trace of makeup and undoubtedly never had, was stolen from Whistler's mother.

Well, I thought, *there goes one little skater dude. This old battle-ax will whisk him out with the rest of the rubbish.*

Nothing could have been further from what happened. Slipping her ample arm around his shoulders, Carrie Nation firmly corralled Snoop-Doggy-Dogg and steered him into the pew beside her. I watched in humbled fascination as she tenderly shared her Bible, then guided his uninitiated eyes through the antique mysteries of a hymn book.

Later I found her in the lobby of the church and inquired after the boy. "Was that your grandson?"

Horror, absolute horror captured her face. "God forbid! Whatever made you think so?"

"Please don't be offended. You were just so kind and loving to sit with him and make him feel comfortable. I just—well, I thought maybe..."

Her eyes twinkled with a devilish merriment at my obvious discomfort, and I knew in a flash this old thing was not nearly as sober and humorless as she looked.

"No," she said, "he's not my grandson, but he's somebody's grandson."

How surprising, how utterly delightful to discover in so unlikely a place, in a church after all, a holiness saint still eager to raise the dead, quite unafraid of a little spiked hair, and so filled with love. In a church yet! What a pleasant surprise!

Where the Spirit of the Lord is, there is liberty—and all kinds of other good stuff, such as creativity, infinite creativity, for one thing. When Elisha saw that small corpse lying there on his bed, no seminary lecture from Methods of Ministry 101 came to mind. He remembered no neatly packaged seminar on raising the dead taught by experts in the field.

This was new ground, a challenge in ministry he had never before encountered. To climb up on the bed and recline himself on the body, to press his face to the very face of the dead, that was an untried approach, a fresh method for a new era. Horrified by the death in the room, Elisha could have fled. Likewise, pinioned by traditional methods he would have been impotent.

When we make methodology into theology we create idols that become limitations on our present and curses on our future. The asinine argument raging through evangelical circles relative to the so-called "seeker sensitive" movement is nothing but bickering over methods, and frequently both sides are sinfully wrong.

Some on the more creative side of the aisle are so lost in the euphoria of their own unusual methods that they have forgotten what it is they are supposed to be about. Being on the cutting edge is not the point; raising the dead is. Elisha did not open a resurrection clinic or mass market his new method. It worked there, once, in that moment. That was enough for Elisha. He forgot neither child nor mother in his rush to get his teaching materials to market. "Call this Shunammite and tell her to come get her son."

By the same token, traditionalists indulge themselves in the luxury of guarding the flame while the naked wait for warmth. Once great methods, ideas that were wildly creative in their day, are now useless antiques in many places. One leader claimed that churches who canceled Sunday night services were denying their heritage and failing their Lord. Oh, please! If Sunday night services work, use them. On the other hand, if the horse dies—dismount!

When poisonous serpents came among the children of Israel, God gave Moses an extraordinary directive. This was a new method, one which was creative, theologically edgy, and magnificently effective. For a brass serpent to be fashioned and lifted up hardly seems appropriate to a people who had been severely punished for making a golden calf. The difference between the golden calf and the brass serpent was neither in metallurgy nor in animal husbandry. The golden calf was their idea; the brass serpent was God's idea, and it was never to be idolized. When, in subsequent generations, it became an idol called Nehushtan, it had to be destroyed. This year's creative concepts of ministry can become next year's idols.

CHAPTER 9

CEMETERY MAINTENANCE

T HERE IS a risk to raising the dead, complications. Raising the dead can get sloppy. Traditionalists addicted to funereal peace and quiet will find the atmosphere around a resurrection disquieting. There is no less stressful ministry than cemetery maintenance; just mow around the graves and keep the headstones clean. Everyone is always present, and all are in tidy rows. There is no bickering, no opinions of any kind, and no one leaves angry.

Just let the dead come alive, however, and they can get rowdy. The problem with raising the dead is the kind of dead who get raised. All the nice dead people, those dead in religion and buried in clean, traditional graves seldom, if ever, come out. It's the dead in their sins who walk out with their grave clothes still on. The street dead, the wounded dead, the dirty dead—when they are raised, they do not know how to act in cemeteries. They expect a party, and they think everybody is supposed to have fun. They may not always dress right for funerals, and it takes a while for dead churches to pound the colorful into conformity.

Imagine the scene at Bethany's synagogue on the Saturday after Lazarus' resurrection. In the first place, it was packed. It was not Jesus alone everyone wanted to see and hear, but Lazarus as well. They wanted to hear his report, to know what death is like and how it felt to come alive again after four days in the grave.

Shall we entertain the thought that Lazarus shuffled reluctantly to his feet after much coaxing, mumbled some half-baked testimony of God's goodness, and, flushed with embarrassment, slumped back into his seat? I think not. I am weary of the weary. I grow wearier yearly at timid saints with tepid testimonies, the half-raised who show little sign that the Lord is risen in them.

I am confident that on the Sabbath day with all of Bethany gathered in the synagogue, Lazarus' testimony of God's grace and power was unrestrained. I can envision the light in his eyes and the radiance of his countenance as he talked. My imagination surveys the faces of the listeners as well. They are not the bored and the duty bound counting the seconds until they can flee the scene for food and fellowship. They are captured, seized by Lazarus' story, uplifted by his joyful gratitude, and awestruck at God's power. The Resurrection and the Life had come to the synagogue with Lazarus, and they were riveted.

Dead men preaching dead messages to dead congregations, zombie churches having lost the joy of being raised from the dead, need more than a fresh touch. A resurrection, *the Resurrection,* is all that can save the situation.

The advantage that Lazarus had was nothing more or less than experience. The resurrection of Christ, like every other doctrine, must not be doctrine alone. Evangelicals love to label liberal churches as the dead ones. Perhaps they are, but churches that are dead right are no more alive than churches that are dead wrong. When experiential Christianity gives up the ghost, a paranoid defensiveness inevitably takes its place.

The "liberals" fear the resurrection because, having barricaded themselves behind a demythologized, warm, and fuzzy so-called "faith," they would not care to see a real Jesus, raised from a real grave, arrive with real power. Why? Because He might just expect to be really obeyed, really believed in, and really preached. Such a Jesus would be very inconvenient in a liberal church where His own words, words such as "born again," have become embarrassing antiques.

Likewise, a resurrected Christ or even a resurrected Lazarus for that matter might prove awkward at many "conservative" bastions of traditionalism. What if Jesus should show up at a church supper with a hooker in tow? What if Jesus suggested that we dismiss church and reconvene at some graveyard where there are more likely corpses? No, better to preach about a well-balanced, well-groomed, conservative Jesus than to risk the release of resurrection power. The Pharisees in the first century could not control Jesus. Neither can the ones in the twenty-first century.

The problem with people like Jesus and Lazarus is that when they play church, they cannot be counted on to play nice. It was not barkeeps and brothel owners who crucified Christ. It was men who loved God's law more than they loved God. Men with religion and no resurrection are dangerous men, lethal in their desire to seal the tomb shut on Christ and everybody else.

Pharisees bribed the guards to lie about the resurrection of Messiah and tried to kill Lazarus.

RESURRECTION

Pharisees still plot and scheme to keep control of the situation. Batten down the hatches. Calm Lazarus down. If this resurrection thing gets out of hand, we may never get it quiet again.

It is a bizarre irony that the liberals and traditionalists often find unity at the resurrection. Liberals don't want the dead raised at all, and conservatives want it done only in certain ways. Liberals lost their faith in the resurrection and created politically correct methods of ministry to reflect a dead theology. Conservatives made idols of their methods and built theologically correct fortresses to keep out the dead.

Lazarus had been to synagogue every Sabbath of his life, but one Saturday morning the resurrection came to synagogue. It was not the synagogue who came to Lazarus in the grave. It was Lazarus, fresh from the grave, who came to the synagogue. Lord, let it be so again. Send us a few Lazaruses fresh from the tomb. Having awakened them, send them to awaken us.

Many years ago, I pastored a small church that was experiencing a spiritual and numerical resurgence. New life, new folks, and new converts packed the pews. It was an exciting season of growth and challenges. Not the least of these

100

challenges was the fifth-grade boys' Sunday school class. These five little darlings were wild as March hares. Virtually uncontrollable, they went through Sunday school teachers like Grant went through Richmond. When it came time for vacation Bible school and no one in their right mind volunteered to spend an entire week in the inferno, the director decided not to have a class for them. I, of course, vetoed this decision, infuriating the director. She announced that finding the teacher for the five demoniacs was now my responsibility.

I thought of a woman named Margaret who was among our most recent converts. The director was horrified at my suggestion.

"She's only been a Christian for six weeks!"

"That may be good for this lot," I countered.

"Her husband is a gangster!" she exclaimed. "I mean it. A gun-toting gangster. Pastor, you have to believe me. Her husband is the real thing. You're new here. That man is a dangerous criminal."

"Perfect," I shouted. "The wife of a mobster will not be intimidated by our five hellions."

Seeing no better option and unhappily facing my determination to teach the boys, she reluctantly yielded but demanded that I be the one to ask Margaret to serve. Furthermore, I was informed that the results of the whole sordid business were my responsibility. The recently converted wife of a gangster in charge of, or in league with, five boys who had reduced grown men to tears was a plan destined for disaster, and she wanted no part of it.

Managing to visit Margaret when her gangster husband was not at home, I sat with her at her kitchen table and enjoyed some cold lemonade and the winsome newness of her relationship with Christ. She teared up as she told me that her few weeks as a Christian had been her happiest. Not having a background in the church, it was all new and exciting to her.

"Margaret," I said at last, "I have come with some great news. The Lord has a job for you."

"For me? The Lord has a job for me?" Her humble amazement was touching. I almost felt guilty about throwing this new Christian into the den of small lions at the church. Almost.

"Yes, Margaret. He wants you to teach the fifth-grade boys in vacation Bible school."

Wonder and delight filled her eyes. "Vacation Bible school! That sounds wonderful." Her initial awe was impressive but quickly faded into concern and confusion. "Pastor, I don't know what that is. I'm new in church, and I've never heard of vacation Bible school."

"Perfect," I said. "All I want is three things. Love these little boys and teach them to love Jesus. I want them to hate the devil. Finally, I want you to win the attendance prize."

Her eyes lit up at that. "Attendance prize? What's that about?"

"The winning class gets to make a special presentation at parents' night."

"What kind of presentation?"

"Oh, like a song, maybe."

"I like that," she said. "I know a good song for little boys."

There are some things you learn in leadership as you gain experience. One of those is to ask questions, but I did not know that then.

On the first day of vacation Bible school, I discovered Margaret and her gang playing army in the church cemetery. A middle-aged woman in a plastic army helmet, toting a toy M-16 is a ludicrous sight, but her tiny soldiers were delighted. The next day her five had become eight, and by week's end Margaret's highly disciplined commando unit of thirty-five had, of course, captured the prize.

RESURRECTION

On parents' night, the small sanctuary was packed. The second-grade girls, daisy petals taped to their necks, sang, "I'm a sunbeam for Jesus," and the first graders could not have been cuter belting out "Zaccheus was a wee little man."

None, however, were as unforgettable as the fifth-grade boys who marched ferociously to the platform with helmets on and weapons shouldered.

"Who do we love?" Margaret barked like a Marine drill instructor.

"Je-sus!" The thirty-five sounded like one hundred.

"Who do we hate?"

"The de-vil!"

"What do we do when we see the devil?"

The boys dropped dramatically to their knees, aimed their plastic guns, and fired at will—a veritable roar of childish throats screaming "Rat-tat-tat-tat!" and spraying imaginary bullets at the unseen enemy of their souls.

"Cease fire!" their leader screamed. "Ten-tion!"

Their devotion to Jesus and their murderous hatred for the devil was equally matched by their submission to a gray-haired woman in a purple dress and an army helmet.

"Ready...sing!" she commanded.

And sing they did:

> Had a little monkey
> Sent him to the country
> Fed him on ginger bread
> Along came a choo-choo,
> Knocked him cuckoo
> Now my monkey's dead.

We gaped. After a few moments we applauded, trying to convince ourselves that the spiritual application of their song was clear to all. Of course, it was not at all clear, but they needn't have been, because the song was not the point. Margaret's creativity was the point. To raise the dead in this post-Christian era we will need the newly raised. Musty methods and musty ministries do not for resurrections make. To creatively reach today's neo-pagans we need some who were pagans recently enough to remember what it was like, grateful enough to still be happy in their faith, and unfettered by the chains of traditional methodologies.

CHAPTER 10

THE DEAD IN CHRIST

RUCIFIED WITH Christ we also share in the
life of His resurrection. Paul put it this
way, "I am crucified with Christ: nevertheless I
live; yet not I, but Christ liveth in me: and the
life which I now live...I live by the [power] of
[him] who loved me, and gave himself for me"
(Gal. 2:20).

Death does not, cannot, separate us from the
love of God in Christ Jesus. Likewise, it does
not, cannot, separate us from the resurrection of
Christ in His body, the church. I refuse to believe
that all the folks who loved me and prayed for
me, who were such a spiritual resource to me
and through whom I experienced the resurrection power of Christ, are completely lost to me
by death. Can death and the grave silence their
prayers and separate me from their love? I refuse
to accept that proposition.

Once in a season of deep need, my wife had
a wonderful vision. Years ago when we were
young, just at the end of the Bronze Age, she was

the fatigued, overworked, overstressed wife of a poverty-stricken young preacher and the mother of two babies under the age of three. One day the maelstrom was on the verge of sucking her under when a marvelous thing happened. The walls around her disappeared, and in their place, all around her, were cheering throngs. Applauding, encouraging her with shouts of affirmation, they urged her on.

"You can do it!"

"Don't give up now."

"You're doing great."

"Hold on to God. Hold on to God!"

Who were they? The body of Christ. At least, her cheering section of it. The point is that from them, through that vision, a young mom was lifted and empowered. It was a turning point in Alison's life and in our understanding of what it means that we are "compassed about with so great a cloud of witnesses" (Heb. 12:1).

At times when I am preaching, especially in the third world, I have been overpoweringly aware, at a level beyond mere memory, of Jim Mann, who introduced me to missions before he died many years ago. Do not be confused. I am not speaking of communing with the dead. God forbid! I do not see ghosts, and I do not hear the voices of the deceased.

I *do*, however, believe that their lives, His life me-ward through them cannot be cut off by death. Their heritage, their teaching, their wonderful words of comfort come to me like the fragrance of honeysuckle on a soft, southern breeze. Those who counseled me, taught me, and spent time on their knees in prayer for me, now in heaven, are now *more* alive, not less. Do they pray in heaven? Why not? If the bowls of incense in heaven are the prayers of the saints, then could those prayers not be for me? Death cannot steal my loved ones. In heaven they know more about the power of the resurrection than I will know until I am there myself.

Now I am confined by the temporal. My body is ruled by laws I cannot yet escape. Gravity, age, and time press heavily on my flesh, and apart from the return of Christ, my days will end in death. Someday I will die. So also will those I love. Yet I also know that through His resurrection, we who believe share a life of prayer and hope that lives beyond the grave. I may grieve, but I cannot be overwhelmed by grief.

Our tears, our sense of loss at the deaths of

loved ones, are real and no shame. We miss them. We long to see them again. Yet we know that they know what we do not. They now live and pray in unconfinement, free of all restraint. They now see our babyhood, the infancy in which we live and think. The dead in Christ *understand* that a freeing and maturing of the spirit is the true nature of death for believers. They understand because they have experienced it. Death has set them free. Our grief is for ourselves, not for them.

It is like this. A mother leaves her infant alone in its bassinette for a few moments. "I am going to the next room to change clothes. I will be *right back*."

The baby begins to cry the minute she leaves the room. He cannot understand. His view of space and time are an infant's. He doesn't know the difference between five minutes and five decades. All he knows is that his mother is out of sight, and to him, out of sight means gone. The next room is the same as another continent, another world, or a different galaxy. All he knows is that she is some other place, some faraway elsewhere, never to be seen again.

In the next room, changing her clothes, she

loves him no less and is no less alive. She hears his tears and pities him, but she is not panic-stricken. She knows that he will be all right and that his baby tears, though sad, are temporary. She is not calloused or uncaring. She simply knows more than he does. She understands time, different rooms, and changes of clothes as he cannot.

Our loved ones who have died in the Lord have stepped into a different room to change clothes. They still live, still love us, and still pray. We can still be touched by their memory, compassed about and bolstered by their intercession, and quieted by their nearness. The resurrection of Christ has made it clear. The dead in Christ are not all that far from those who live in Christ.

They who have stepped through the door of death understand what we cannot, and they would comfort us. Listen to their voices. "I am just in the next room changing clothes. I will be right back."

A Resurrection Heritage

The funeral procession wound its way slowly, quietly toward the burial ground. The widow, too young a woman for this tragedy, wept softly as she walked. Those around her spoke only in whispers. Above the grieving knot of mourners, on the ridge that jutted eastward like the spine of a beast, an armed sentry kept vigil. Glancing only now and again at the procession below and behind him, the warrior peered anxiously into the eastern wilderness.

Across the river loomed the ominous purple mountains of Moab. Down from these rugged hills, bent on slaughter and pillage, ferocious raiders, Moabites without mercy, came in small bands to attack any easy target. This was not war, army against army, but lightning fast guerilla raids that hit hard, killing or capturing everyone on some isolated farm or small village before melting back into Moab's harsh terrain. These murderous raiders were greatly feared, and Israel's only safety was in numbers.

A funeral such as this one would be easy prey. The lone sentry was hired security, paid by the day as part of the funeral expense to watch and cry out at the first sight of danger. Even as heavily armed as he was, a single man would be no match for a band of Moabites, and the mourners had no desire either to carry weapons or hire a full force sufficient to handle a raiding party.

Getting quickly back into the city was deemed sufficient protection, so one experienced lookout was hired.

The veteran on the ridge saw movement long before he could really discern what it was. His name was Reuben, and he was known for his vision as well as his diligence. Hardly able to see a tapestry pattern he held in his own hands, Reuben could pick out an ibex at high altitude before anyone else could even see a white spot. Against the distant hills across the river not yet clearly identifiable, Reuben picked out movement and knew he could not afford to wait too long. Tightening the grip on his spear, he kept his eyes trained on the spot.

Seven, no eight, he could count them now, and he was certain they were not deer or camels. These were mounted men riding single file like warriors, and they were headed for the river. Reuben estimated the Moabites would soon be across the river and close enough to see the funeral. If the Moabites managed to get between the mourners and the city gate, slaughter would be the result. Not wanting to cry out, Reuben scrambled down from his rocky perch and whispered the bad news to several men on the outskirts of the procession. The effect was immediate.

Despite the protests of the near-hysterical widow, all plans for the funeral were summarily dropped. Moabite raiders in sight left no room for debate and no time for mourning. The nearest tomb, though occupied, was easily and quickly accessible. Its famous occupant would hardly object. Even a dead prophet is dead, and dead men do not care about being crowded. As for the new corpse, he would not complain either. Expediency made the decision for them all.

The sobbing widow was still complaining that this was not right and that the Moabites would not see them if they would only be quiet. The women gathered around her comfortingly, but the men ignored her protests. Elisha had been a great man, a prophet of great power, but dead was dead and one man more or less in Elisha's tomb would make no difference. Right now the living were more important than dead prophets or dead husbands, and right now the living had to be saved from the Moabites.

The stone was quickly rolled away, and three burly fellows carried the dead man in. It was a single tomb despite Elisha's notoriety. On the carved stone resting place lay the linen-wrapped remains of the prophet. There was no other place. Their hearts were pounding. They felt stranded, trapped between the death in the tomb and the death outside with the Moabites. Avoiding each other's eyes, they unceremoniously deposited their burden on the prophet's corpse and beat a hasty retreat.

Outside the three pallbearers were greeted with downcast eyes like defeated soldiers returning from a lost war. The men shifted from foot to foot in awkward silence, and the women cooed and petted at the weeping widow. Someone murmured that they had best get back, and as others softly, but eagerly, agreed, the shuffling of sandaled feet on the rocky path became the only sound among the tombs.

Suddenly the young widow screamed. Pandemonium, noisy confusion instantly spread through the little knot. No one gave the Moabites a thought. Astonishment, a mixed cloud of awe and fear and incredulous joy engulfed them. The Moabites disappeared behind the wall of the miraculous moment. Standing there, as alive as they were, was the dead husband.

114

The widow, a widow no more, sobbed in joy, "Is it you? Are you alive?"

"Yes," said her husband, and he spread his arms to embrace her. "I am."

"The Lord is God," she cried, rushing into his embrace.

"Yes," he said. "The Lord is God."

*   *   *

Behind us, behind each of us, remaining after we make our exit, is what is called heritage, a legacy of life or death. Even from beyond the grave, lives can be touched, will be touched. The power of His life within us can grant us the power of resurrection ministry even after our own death.

A life lived in the power of His life is a witness that cannot be silenced. Lives of grace, lives raised from the dead by Christ's love, reach up from the tomb to raise the dead. The prayers of the saintly grandmother, the inheritance of a Christian dad, the sermons of an anointed pastor—these live on. These are the body of Elisha. Whatever is laid on them finds life.

Likewise, men who lived lives of death leave legacies of death. A friend of mine did a stretch in prison before he found the Lord. His father came to visit him there and made an ironic announcement. Years earlier the father had worked on the construction crew that had built the prison. Many a son has lived in prisons built by their fathers, yet a legacy of death and bondage can be broken by the name and blood of Jesus. We are not condemned to live in the prisons built by the dead. On the other hand, why must those prisons be built at all?

We can instead be prophets of life upon whose bodies the generations to come can be laid to come alive. The sermons of Wesley still speak. The anointing of Seymour lives. The legacy of Billy Graham will go on and on in ever-widening circles of life and influence. Likewise, unknowns, unsung saints have built houses of blessing, not prisons of death and bondage. What is laid upon such lives will experience an inheritance of resurrection power.

For more information about Global Servants or to receive a product list of the many books, audio and video tapes, CDs and DVDs by Mark Rutland, write, call, or go online:

Global Servants
1601 Williamsburg Square
Lakeland, FL 33803
(888) 823-8772 (Toll Free)
www.globalservants.org

The Rutland Group offers leadership and church growth consultancies and cohort educational experiences for more information write or call:

Global Servants
1601 Williamsburg Square
Lakeland, FL 33803
(888) 823-8772 (Toll Free)

For more information about Southeastern University write, call, or go online:

Southeastern University
1000 Longfellow Blvd
Lakeland, FL 33801
(863) 667-5000 (Main Number)
www.seuniversity.edu